THE BUSINESS OF SPORTS TECHNOLOGY

The BUSINESS *of* SPORTS TECHNOLOGY

How to Make Smart Decisions That Drive Your Organization Forward

DAVID NUGENT

www.amplifypublishinggroup.com

The Business of Sports Technology: How to Make Smart Decisions That Drive Your Organization Forward

For more information, please contact:
Sports Business Journal Publishing, an imprint of Amplify Publishing Group
620 Herndon Parkway, Suite 220
Herndon, VA 20170
info@amplifypublishing.com

Library of Congress Control Number: 2025919373

CPSIA Code: PRV1125A

ISBN-13: 979-8-89138-359-3

Printed in the United States

To my wife, Jeanine, and children, Reece, Hudson, and Tess—

Your love, encouragement, and unwavering belief in me made this possible.

CONTENTS

INTRODUCTION

In 2014, we were hired to help a large sports media company with a very visible technology project in distress.

The sports media company had decided to invest in a new enterprise-level content management system (CMS) with the goal of increasing publishing velocity, generating more ad revenue, and syndicating content to sister companies. Their old CMS had become antiquated, and with frequent issues creating operational and financial stress, doing nothing was no longer an option. Content creation and delivery were key to their business model; in fact, this *was* their business model. Unfortunately, when we were brought in, the deployment was in serious trouble. The project was late and millions over budget, and the executive who hired us was under tremendous pressure to course-correct. His job depended on getting the platform up and running soon.

As our team was being onboarded, the executive told me frankly that he believed the technology they'd chosen was at fault.

We analyzed the situation, and I found (as expected) that he was wrong. We've overseen incredibly successful, on-time deployments of the exact technology his company chose in other organizations. It's a leading solution in the field for content management and was a good choice for this company's goals.

The company had a people and process problem, not a technology one. First, the people: His team had no experience with the technology, and an agency that had been brought in to assist with design did not either. There was also an issue with governance. Responsibility was not well defined, with many parts of the project left without clear owners and too many team members unclear on who was in charge. Perhaps most concerning (to me at least) was the approach to execution, specifically project management. The company was trying to manage an enterprise-level project with a profound lack of process. The project plan lacked critical detail and resource planning was an afterthought. They had the software to monitor individuals' work and the progress of the project against milestones, but they weren't using it.

In sports businesses, rigorous project planning is not optional. We live in a world where delivery dates can't change. So, if a project falls behind even a little bit, issues must be identified and corrected immediately, or small problems will compound to big ones. Because this company had gaps in process and planning, by the time they noticed a problem, they were too far along to correct it without a large-scale mess, which is what they had when we arrived. Making things worse, because the project had diffuse governance, even if they *had* noticed a problem early, it might remain unsolved because everyone assumed someone else was in charge of fixing it.

While there is such a thing as bad technology, I have rarely seen an enterprise-level project go wrong because of the technology products themselves. Usually the issue is a people and process one. Someone chose the wrong technology for the outcome needed or deployed it using the wrong people or processes, or both. I often describe this reality by asking an executive to imagine someone trying to hammer a large nail into a block of wood with a small Phillips-head screwdriver. It won't work—but that's not because Phillips-head screwdrivers don't work. It's because they are not made for hammering nails!

Of course, even when organizations choose the correct technology for their needs, they may struggle to develop, deploy, and manage it without the right team or the right plan. It doesn't mean the teams are not competent; they simply do not have the requisite experience in the selected technologies or in the processes required to deliver the right results on time and in budget.

Fortunately, my team had the right experience and process to rescue this project. Our client was ultimately able to use the chosen CMS to deliver content and generate revenue with all the features and control needed. And the executive was able to save the project and his job, letting him learn and grow to deploy future technology more smoothly.

CRITICAL DECISIONS

Technology decisions are among the biggest bets a sports organization will ever make. They're expensive and therefore high stakes—there are rarely do-overs for the largest decisions, and they all carry ongoing costs. Technology has also become core to the revenue goals and very identity of sports organizations. Getting it right keeps fans engaged, partners happy, and should provide revenue streams that are otherwise unavailable. Getting it wrong is a visible and dangerous black eye for the brand.

Of course, all of this is complicated by the pace of change and the realities of the industry. The need to constantly assess new technologies means decisions become exponentially more complex over time. And every sports executive lives in a world of limits. There is always more work to do than resources and more things to buy than there is budget. Fans have high expectations that are constantly changing, and—unlike in other industries—launch dates in sports cannot and will not move.

Given all the layered challenges, how do sports executives keep up with the pace of change? How do they make *smarter* technology decisions to deliver more with bigger payoffs that take into account their constraints?

To begin with, it's nearly impossible for one person to keep pace with technological change alone. The role of the sports executive, then, I would argue, is to remain focused on the *business* of their specific sport—baseball, football, hockey, gymnastics, or sailing, for example—and to look elsewhere for expertise on specific technologies. They should surround themselves with trusted advisors whose job is to ensure that the executive has the information they need to make the right decisions for their situation. The advisors can operate from within the organization, or external to it; in many cases, organizations will be best served by having good internal advisors as well as external consultants with different specialties.

Technology is a tool, not a destination. **Rather than starting a major technology decision with a list of technologies, start with**

business goals. Once you know where you are going, *then* you can select the technology and plan your execution accordingly.

THE QUESTIONS TO ASK

Before selecting technical solutions, ask questions like the following.

- What outcome are we trying to achieve?
- What do we want the technology to do toward that end?
- When we're done, how do we know it worked?

Although the questions may seem obvious, simple questions aren't asked or answered nearly enough in technology decisions. People will sometimes spend millions getting an app or other technology offering, with no path whatsoever to monetization.

Of course, being innovative in public *can be* a viable business strategy in sports. Partners love the brand lift of enabling innovative technologies, and fans can love those technologies if they are well executed. Even here, however, big technology decisions must be married back to business outcomes. Smart executives will also plan for how to measure whether the innovative technology has accomplished the business goals. Otherwise, they're just spending money with no clear criteria for if (or when) to spend that money again.

Technology, just like every other investment, needs to pay for itself in terms of revenue, fan engagement, or other value.

DECISIONS MATTER

With technology becoming more complex and the stakes becoming ever higher, getting technology decisions right has become mission critical for sports organizations. It's not complicated, but it's hard. In other words, there's a process to a result that is not complex but also not easy to execute well.

The rest of the book will lay out a framework to help you connect your business goals to the right technology—and support smarter decisions. Then, I'll walk you through some current technology options at a high level and tell you where emerging tech is likely going. Throughout, I'll focus on the strategy behind good decision-making in sports technology and continually pull it back to you and your organization's needs. While I won't tell you exactly what to do at any point, I will try to outline how to approach smarter decisions and how to plan out the journey in a way that makes getting to your goals far more likely. I'll also highlight how to manage risk and take advantage of opportunities for revenue as we go.

WHAT I WILL NOT COVER

Success in technology rests on a trifecta: being able to (1) choose the right technology for the situation, (2) plan how that technology will be built, deployed, and operated, and then (3) implement that plan well, with solid project management and excellent execution. I will only cover the first two topics in this book.

There are a few reasons I neglect the third topic. Perhaps the easiest is length; the book is long enough without including the details that would be required to properly cover the successful technology execution. This would make this book much more technical and much less interesting to business people. If you can get through the right decisions on which technologies to choose (and why) and have the right plan for how it will be built, deployed, and operated, resources (internally or externally) can be engaged to follow your plan and execute.

Poorly architecting systems and writing bad code are big problems, but they're not ones that I will cover in this book. So, if your team has any weaknesses in execution, you should address those by hiring outside partners to supplement your internal capabilities.

WHO I AM

I should probably tell you at this point that I have a degree in English literature, not computer science or engineering. While I have run technology services businesses for many years, my day-to-day work is business and commercial, as highlighted in my other book, *Zero Sales*. While some people might argue that my lack of an engineering background should disqualify me from writing a book about technology, I believe the opposite: It's because of my background that I am the right person to write this book.

Rather than approaching technology from an engineering perspective, I approach it practically. I care about the details of tech, but I focus primarily on how technology helps sports organizations make money. That's why this book is called *The "Business" of Sports Technology*. In a battle between business goals and flashy technology, I'll choose the business goals every time. So should you.

Experience is the second—and more important—reason to listen to me. I've worked in technology since the mid-nineties, and I've been in sports technology since 2003, during which time I've secured and helped service hundreds of technology projects. Because of that experience, I have a very broad (but not necessarily very deep) perspective on a wide variety of topics in sports technology. This is what I do every single day at work: explaining technology to business people and business to technology people. I will do the same for you in this book.

Sports Technology

The sports industry—including technology in sports—is unique. Because I have consulted on and deployed tech on time for organizations across sports, I have become intimately familiar with the specific requirements and realities of sports technology and the processes we have to adopt to meet those challenges. No matter how technical someone's background is, if they have limited subject matter expertise in sports and don't understand how to run a project where the date cannot move, their advice will not be useful for the sports industry.

Because sports are different, the so-called technology best practices from other industries are often not our best practices. For example, something like traditional Agile development won't work here without modifications (i.e., Agile sprints within a waterfall framework), because the launch date cannot move. Sports require a specific set of disciplines to ensure the finish line is crossed on time and within budget, with systems that behave as expected. The process and planning must work, full stop.

WHY I WROTE THIS BOOK

Providing technology services to the sports industry is a very specific niche, and I've had a long career doing it. Over time, I've noticed patterns. I've developed philosophies and established rules that were helpful as we went into new engagements. I've overseen many talented team members who helped develop the processes that bring projects in on time, in budget, and with working software in an unforgiving landscape. Over time, we've also shared these ideas with clients, whom we've learned from and who have given helpful feedback. Now I feel there's value in sharing this experience with the world. You'll see that this book leverages the thought leadership of many high-profile sports industry executives and that its philosophies are not just mine but the aggregate of years of sharing and learning.

When I was new to the sports industry, I knew very little. The people who shared their knowledge with me made a tremendous impact; the patterns and advice they gave me became helpful every single day until I experienced enough to create my own understanding. Now, as I look back at a professional career in a specific niche, I'd like to help others. I'd like to provide value as value was provided to me.

A GUIDE FOR THE REST OF THE BOOK

Here's what to expect from the rest of the book. In part one, I will walk you through the building blocks of strategic decision-making in the business of sports technology. Chapters one and two comprise the foundational thinking I find organizations too often leave out. I strongly recommend you read these sections carefully and work through the recommended thinking for an upcoming decision your organization must make. Each chapter contains examples of sports organizations who make very different kinds of decisions based on their identities and values (chapter one) and their goals as an organization (chapter two). These examples will help you understand how to apply the principles to your situation.

Chapters three through five serve as connecting chapters, as I show you how to translate your organization's goals and the decision you have made into a tactical, near-term plan. These chapters include information about how to assess different technology options and make smart decisions in implementation based on your needs. In the last chapter of this part (five), I emphasize the need to take steps to plan for inevitable challenges ahead of time to decrease the risk of failure.

In part two, I will move to a more granular approach. Rather than strategy, this section will give you the lay of the land when it comes to the major categories of off-field technology currently in use in sports organizations. In order, the chapters cover:

- partnerships and advertising
- fan data and marketing technology
- venue and events
- media technologies

I will rarely give you specific brand names in these chapters and never specific recommendations for which to choose. Instead, I will give you a high-level understanding of each category and guide you in how to think about choosing and deploying technology. I will give you the *why* and the *how* of good decision-making in that category. I do not focus on specific technology brands since this information quickly goes out of date, and I assume that you can either do your own technology product research or can hire someone to do it for you.

Lastly, I use chapter ten to discuss emerging technologies in sports. I walk you through where I and several leading thinkers in sports technology believe we are going in the future.

MANAGING EXPECTATIONS

As you may have spotted, I will be covering many categories of "off-the-field" technology in sports, the ones that affect business operations performance on the P&L. There are other incredible sports technologies affecting "on-the-field" performance, but this book won't cover them. Instead, I will approach technology through a business lens, highlighting how to use technology to generate revenue, limit risk, create efficiency, and build the fan relationships that ultimately drive the business of sports.

BEGIN AT THE BEGINNING

If you don't know where you are going,
any road will get you there.

—Lewis Carroll

Unfortunately, I talk to businesses on a regular basis who don't know where they're going. They have few goals beyond collecting the money from today. I ask them what matters to them when it comes to technology, how they think about innovation, and what role tech should play in their business, and they don't know. That makes it very difficult to deliver technology that will drive their business forward. They don't know what *forward* looks like.

Business, like every other part of life, is about what's next. (That's why we called our company *Next League*—we're focusing on what's next.) Businesses create strategies, set goals, define revenue targets, and establish key performance indicators in every other area, milestones to show the direction everyone should pull. Why not in technology? Why choose a tactic before choosing the outcome it is supposed to drive? That doesn't make any sense.

Technology is a tool, a path to an outcome, and ideally not just any outcome. The best and most effective deployments of technology advance your overall business direction. So I will begin this book at the beginning: with who you are and where you are as a sports organization. The *outcomes*, and the technology you choose to obtain them, fall naturally from there.

PART ONE

BUILDING YOUR STRATEGY

1

WHO ARE YOU?

On February 1, 2014, Adam Silver began his tenure as NBA commissioner, and he faced a dilemma. Social media had become global, and social platforms like Twitter and Instagram had become the world's water cooler. Conversations about NBA news, players, and games were taking place among both fans and NBA players. The issue was game highlight videos were being widely shared on these platforms.

Technically, only rightsholders and those who had purchased rights could legally share or distribute those video highlights. In fact, a significant portion of major sports leagues wanted to immediately shut that sharing down, as they worried that the highlights may hurt their broadcast viewership or, perhaps worse, imperil their rights deals.

Of course, media rights deals are incredibly valuable and core to the business model of all large sports leagues. Shortly after

Silver's start as commissioner, the NBA announced a nine-year, $24 billion deal that was to run through the 2024–25 season.

The NBA and all other major sports leagues had a strategic decision to make: try to stop the distribution of this protected content IP (which included rights-protected highlights and images) on social media or let it spread all over the internet. Many sports industry executives were initially in favor of trying to shut down the sharing. Allowing the content might mean killing the goose that laid the golden eggs, causing irreparable damage to the entire business model. Sports leagues had justifiable trepidation.

Silver, however, had a different view. He paid attention to the fact that NBA players had already embraced these platforms as a way to share their opinions and build their personal brands. Players like Blake Griffin and Kyrie Irving were sharing their thoughts (and GIFs) on Twitter and Instagram.* Silver recognized that fan engagement with the content was significant. Trying to shut it down entirely might not be possible and would certainly upset fans. He also had the vision to see that content consumption would not be a zero-sum game—fans who saw the highlights, if anything, might be driven to the games in larger numbers.

Silver made the NBA's position clear as one of the first voices to embrace the new model—the NBA would not only allow highlights to be viewed on social platforms, but they would encourage the practice. As Silver said in a *Wall Street Journal* article at the time, "The games are the meals and the highlights are the snacks,

* DeJohn, Kenny. 2016. "NBA Social Media Awards 2014 Results: Tracking Complete List of Winners." *Bleacher Report*, November 5, 2016. https://bleacherreport.com/articles/2102905-nba-social-media-awards-2014-results-tracking-complete-list-of-winners.

and we encourage our fans to snack before meals. But the meals are pristine and the meals live behind a paywall . . . we can help facilitate it." * The NBA had made it clear who they were and what they believed—they were all in on growth and would deliver great experiences to fans.

More than a decade later, the NBA remains a fan-focused and global organization that innovates consistently when it comes to content. They support about half a billion fans worldwide, with the largest social media following of any professional sports league in the world. As Chris Benyarko, EVP, direct-to-consumer products, technology & operations at the NBA, recently told me, "We are supporting a very wide and diverse range of fans . . . across multiple interests and age groups. So innovation is almost critical in order for us to operate."

The NBA has made it clear that *who they are* is a global league that will not only bring the game to the fans, no matter where they are, but also allow those fans to then use content to amplify the NBA brand by building their own followings and crafting their own stories. They invest heavily in innovative technology in the content space to connect with their fans—technology that includes app personalization. The NBA prioritizes technology that will serve the global diversity of their fans. Benyarko highlighted, "Our direct consumer business accepts over 130 different currencies, and provides our pay flow through a lot of different languages."

They also invest heavily in innovative content technology in keeping with who they are. For example, the NBA provides personalization

* Gay, Jason. 2015. "The NBA Climbs the Social Ladder." *The Wall Street Journal*. November 19, 2015. https://www.wsj.com/articles/the-nba-climbs-the-social-ladder-1447976815.

and geolocation on its app, determining each person's interests and preferred formats, and then delivering those consistently. Benyarko continued: "Some people still like to look at traditional two-and-a-half-to-three-minute highlights. And other people want to just swipe through vertical video . . . One of the advantages of having a digital delivery is that you can present the game in almost endless amounts of ways. So, you can have different camera angles, different audio . . . It's not just about different languages, but also how you call the game . . . pop culture element, some of the heavy stat-based stuff, you could also present that." This effective use of personalization means building and appending profiles both implicitly and explicitly. The result is that over time, fans become more engaged with content longer, and more frequently.

The NBA translates its investment in technology and a direct relationship with fans into long-term opportunities for additional revenue. Benyarko noted, "If you participate in the NBA and buy merch, we can also help you participate in playing fantasy. And if you play fantasy, we participate in getting you to go to a game." It's not just about the subscription or sales revenue, however. According to Benyarko, when the organization reaches a fork in the road, it makes decisions based on whatever technology makes it easier to be an NBA fan. Their focus on the fan and the content the fans want and need guides their business. They see the relationship with the fan as their guiding light and know that fostering that relationship will result in growth.

Even before the internet would eventually empower players and fans to share content and exponentially expand their reach, the NBA was focused on being a global brand that would deliver great experiences to fans no matter where they were. They knew who they were and who they wanted to be, and they were willing to invest heavily in technology to get there.

STARTING IN THE RIGHT PLACE

For sports executives working in technology, it can be tempting to take the most direct path to revenue. After all, building meaningful relationships with fans takes time and money, and all sports executives have growth goals. This is where understanding *who you are* comes in. For the NBA, this means focusing on building and managing long-term relationships with fans across the entire spectrum of basketball globally, but this strategy, and the technology that will power it, takes vision and scale.

For many sports executives, the reality of shorter-term goals can often make rushed decisions feel necessary. New technology options surface on a weekly basis. Because each new request for analyzing new technologies feels urgent, the idea of your organization falling behind can create tremendous stress. Resisting the urge to engage with new technology before you can articulate the *why* can be difficult, but starting with the selection of specific technologies without first considering the desired business outcome is the tail wagging the dog.

Rarely do rushed technology decisions work out well for organizations. Instead, the biggest benefits come from an approach centered on knowing who you are as an organization and translating that knowledge into strategic, consistent decisions to drive technology implementation.

DIFFERENT ORGANIZATIONS HAVE DIFFERENT VALUES

Perkins Miller, CEO of PlayOn Sports and formerly CEO of Fandom, has experience across the sports technology world. He's worked on four Olympics, World Wrestling Entertainment (WWE), and the NFL and has seen firsthand the differences in how those three organizations handle technology decisions. Miller highlights the reality that each company tends to focus first on what they're good at and what they know. But "technology is a lot about the unknown . . . Where do you decide to take action?" The way sports organizations decide to take action and for what reasons depends on who they are culturally.

With the Olympics, Miller talked about the constraints of big-picture thinking while managing the reality of budget constraints. "You can't really spend any money yourself, but you can certainly put together a collection of businesses and figure it out . . . If you can be creative and smart about it, you can do what you want. So we put together a deal with Microsoft and half a dozen other companies to put [a mobile platform and social technologies] together in exchange for their promotional value and it worked out great." The Olympics hitched technology to partnerships, and that cultural identity drove which technologies were possible.

In the case of the WWE, the organization had the resources to buy technology that supported their core business—*if* it fit their values of quality and speed. Miller recalled, "[the WWE has] always been willing to hustle. It was like, look, we think we can build a direct-to-consumer streaming platform in the WWE Network. We're willing to take a risk on it. And the trick there culturally was, it had to be really good and has to be really fast, which are two things that tend to be really expensive."

He contrasted that emphasis on speed with the NFL's values of quality and consistency, which are not necessarily less expensive. From his experience, the NFL's cultural identity is "among the top three most prestigious sports brands in the world. They have a different set of conditions. And in their conditions, it's a little better to be right than fast . . . It was about being really thoughtful and strategic and ensuring that what you deliver is of high quality. It doesn't necessarily need to be [fast], but of course you still have to hit the season. The season starts when the season starts."

Each organization makes different technology choices based on different organizational values. You should do the same. Before you decide on a specific technology or technology strategy, don't just determine the obvious identity markers of your organization—your size, age, type of organization, and so on—but also what your values and priorities are.

Who You Are Drives Your Technology Choices

As I described in the introduction, technology is not one-size-fits-all. The right technologies for each business will depend on who they are and what they value. The set of tools perfect for the WWE's hustle and speed might be a fundamental mismatch for an organization that is fundamentally more risk averse.

The technology needs of a sports organization should always start with what is unique about that sport. From that starting place, product strategies can be designed to take advantage of the sport's uniqueness to engage fans in technological ways that were impossible even twenty years ago.

The choice of specific technologies should follow the foundational understanding of the following four dimensions:

1. What the sport is and what it represents on the world stage

2. Who the organization is in terms of values and priorities, including its innovation culture
3. How they will deploy technologies to achieve specific outcomes and how those outcomes will be measured and monitored
4. Where the organization is going in the near future—its business goals for the next three to five years

Dimensions one and two will be covered in this chapter, and three and four will be discussed in more depth in chapter two.

The key idea of this top-down strategy approach to technology is simple: Technology can simultaneously be a great tool and a poor compass. To select the right technologies, you must first know who you are and where you are going.

THE STRUCTURE OF THE ORGANIZATION MATTERS

Unsurprisingly, very large sports organizations tend to have different business goals and technology needs than very small organizations. The proven league business models of older and larger sports organizations can make innovation feel like risk. Conversely, younger and smaller sports organizations may choose to innovate with technology to attract the attention of desired audiences. They have less risk because they have less to lose. Who each organization *is* impacts their technology decisions.

The same goes for an organization's structure. A league will have different priorities and goals than a team. A federation and a national governing body will have different needs and values than a college sports conference. Every group will use technology differently.

Of course, the nature of each sport creates unique challenges, opportunities, and priorities for technology. For example, MLB teams play 162 regular season games a year, with 81 home games. Ticket sales comprise a little over 30 percent of their revenue,[*] and their priorities and technology reflect this reality. The NFL currently gets over 65 percent of its revenue from media rights, all of which are national, so they are very focused on providing an excellent television experience. With a more even distribution of ticket sales and media rights income, the NHL and the NBA balance both business models.[†]

The PGA TOUR regularly hosts one hundred-plus golfers at events over several days. NASCAR is an endurance sport driven by automotive technology, and its races are long with a unique character as a result. Both companies invest in technology that looks different from the large "stick and ball" sports,[‡] and different from each other.

The World Surf League has challenges scheduling TV broadcasts because their events are so dependent on weather and waves.

---

* Badenhausen, Kurt. 2024. "How Sports Teams Leagues and Owners Make Money." *Sportico.com*, February 16, 2024. https://www.sportico.com/feature/how-sports-teams-leagues-make-money-1234766931/.

† Statista. 2024. "NBA Regular Season Ticketing Revenue as Share of Total Revenue 2010-2024." October 25, 2024. https://www.statista.com/statistics/193410/percentage-of-ticketing-revenue-in-the-nba-since-2006

‡ Since I've worked with both organizations for a long time, I use them as examples throughout the book. Because they are different, both from each other and from the traditional leagues, they show the breadth of possibilities for technology in sports.

The same goes to a lesser degree for Sail GP. Each sport has its own benefits and detriments.

Short Windows for Revenue

Most sports are under pressure from a technology point of view since much of their revenue is made in short "live windows." The situation is more stark for some sports than others. The United States Tennis Association (USTA) hosts one event (the US Open) that makes 85 to 90 percent of their revenue for the year, and the situation is similar with the United States Golf Association (USGA) and its U.S. Open. For another example, Sarah Hirshland, the CEO of the United States Olympic & Paralympic Committee (USOPC), likes to joke that, unlike many sports, the Olympics has "a really long offseason." It's two years between summer and winter games, and four between each summer and winter game, respectively. Building constituency and fandom is more challenging in a world where the sport disappears for years at a time, and how the Olympics invests in technology accounts for that long offseason.

The technology that an organization chooses should not be based on what others do but rather its own business model and the needs of its sport.

YOUR IDENTITY AND VALUES

Who the organization *is* and what it values ultimately comes down from leadership. The CEO, commissioner, board of directors, or president pushes the organization in a specific direction, defining its strategy and values. Look at the statements that leaders have put out about your organization. Then, consider the felt reality of how the organization functions. What cultural touchstones are important? What values matter to the organization?

For example, Oak View Group (OVG) manages many large public venues. According to Katee LaPoff, chief technology officer of OVG, sustainability is a key part of their corporate culture: "I think that it is a growing sense of urgency and a growing requirement. And moreover, it's just the right thing to do. Our leader, Tim Leiweke, often says that he wants to leave this planet better for his grandchildren than what he inherited." LaPoff says sustainability drives decisions for the organization at every level.

Your organization may value cost, speed of delivery, speed of innovation, fan relationship, perceived quality, "cool" factor, or any other value. It may have several values or prioritize certain things over others. Make a longer list and narrow it down if needed.

Unfortunately, leadership does change over time, which means your organizational values and priorities may also change over time. Even so, identify who the organization is now, and how that is likely to impact technology decisions, before moving on to the next section. Making decisions in concert with your existing values is always better when facing trade-offs.

YOUR INNOVATION CULTURE

Perhaps no single value or topic will impact your technology decisions and implementations more than your innovation culture. Does your organization prefer conservative approaches to business goals, or does it have the culture to support big risks? Is it bleeding edge, cutting edge, fast follow, follow, or lagging when it comes to technology? How and why does the organization choose to innovate?

Innovation is, by definition, new, and new things carry with them inherent risk. Sometimes, innovation absorbs time and money without returning much in the way of reward. Other times, being first—or on the bleeding or cutting edge—carries with it massive benefits. How an organization measures those benefits also matters to how willing they are to invest again.

Of course, as already discussed, some organizations simply need innovation more than others. Well-established, large organizations with successful business models may not need or want to innovate. Smaller organizations still growing their sport may benefit more from the brand lift of *new*. There is no wrong way to be innovative—or not—so long as decisions on new technology options are made in keeping with an organization's overall culture.

To help you consider how your organization may approach risk and innovation, here are some examples of different organizations and how each chooses to approach the topic.

The Risk-Averse Organization

MLB Advanced Media (MLBAM) created BAMTech as a separate company in 2015, and by 2016, Disney was interested enough in its streaming technology to purchase a 33 percent stake in the company for $1 billion.* Around this time another very large sports organization that we worked with had a similar opportunity. Their senior technology person teamed up with media rights and external technology providers to develop a platform that would serve other sports properties, much in the same way BAMTech had. In the

* "The Walt Disney Company Acquires Minority Stake in BAMTech" The Walt Disney Company. February 6, 2018. https://thewaltdisneycompany.com/the-walt-disney-company-acquires-minority-stake-in-bamtech/.

short term, the bottom-line profit of the plan was estimated to be hundreds of millions of dollars. Despite their plan being both realistic and achievable, the team who presented it was told no, firmly. The senior technology person left shortly thereafter, and the new leader cut most of the technology staff.

To be clear, while this decision was and is risk averse, it's not necessarily wrong. The organization justifiably wanted to focus on its core business—their sport. They might not have been able to execute on the vision in practice. And even if they had, spending time, resources, and focus on another business line might truly have distracted from other key business priorities. Either way, a sizable profit, one that could have grown significantly in time, was dismissed because it didn't align with the culture and vision of the organization. They protected what they had, at the price of what might have been.

The PGA TOUR

The PGA TOUR is an interesting example of a thriving innovation culture. According to Scott Gutterman, SVP digital & broadcast technologies, "One of the things we've always felt . . . which drives a lot of what we do, is we know golf. We know golf really well and we know golf technology really well." And to do both they knew they needed some level of innovation.

Originally, he said, the executive team and board wanted to know how the technology team could "be ahead and lead in sports." The policy had been to attach sponsors to all innovation projects, but the need for a sponsor prevented experimenting with projects that may or may not work. His group pitched an innovation program to the executive team and board: "If you can fund us with this amount of money, we can hire a couple of people . . . to be even more forward looking. And the support for that really came from Commissioner Jay Monahan. They were fully behind it."

After that point, his team could peel off a portion of their innovation budget and experiment to see if an idea worked. Given the sheer quantity of data possible, from how high the balls carry to distance and ball spin, the PGA TOUR has wanted to find ways of measuring that data and making it understandable to fans. The value they placed on stretching the fan experience wouldn't always make money.

Over the years, Gutterman says the innovation program budget led directly to developing technologies "that eventually became monetizable or sponsorable." He continues, "It led to statistics we've been doing for years, and it led to working with companies like WSC Sports and automated video highlight clipping." Eventually the positive impact of the innovation program became so obvious that, counterintuitively, they closed it: "What happened now is that that practice has spread itself among our departments . . . We know that our departments are going to come and ask us to fund things that are going to be for the future. And we need to give them the opportunity . . . And so the reason, the good news is the culture shifted so much that it's adopted that ethos throughout the organization." Every year the PGA TOUR puts money aside specifically for innovation work, and the latitude to experiment has led to big wins.

Other Organizations

NASCAR runs on automotive technology, on the track and beyond. They also invest heavily in digital media experiences. Rather than seeking out innovation for the sake of innovation, they prefer to take the middle of the track by ensuring innovative technology is fully paid for by partners. For example, they have built an augmented reality (AR) experience that allows a car to "drive" around a fan's living room. In another case, fans could look through their phones at a Coke can and enter a fully immersive version of pit road. The emphasis on partnership allows them to innovate without much additional cost, and they continue to deliver the fun and fresh experiences their fans love.

As described in the story that opens this chapter, the NBA has always been on the cutting edge of content delivery despite being a large, established league. At a time when most other big leagues in North America were actively fighting video highlights on social media, the NBA was happy to let the highlights go wide. They had always been a highlight-driven sport; highlights were part of their culture and how they saw their game. Over time, though, their bet paid off big—their business exploded internationally. Other major leagues have followed their lead.

Determine Your Innovation and Risk Culture

Now that you've studied the way that other sports organizations approach risk and innovation, consider where your organization fits in the pack. Will you take on the risk of innovation to set trends, even if that risk does not pay off? Are you content to stick to tried-and-true, cost-effective, and consistent technologies, even at the risk of being behind the curve? Or do you prefer a middle path, where you embrace the right kind of innovation for your brand identity as long as you can attach it to partners?

Your answer might also change depending on the type of technology at play. Some teams will invest cutting-edge tech in venues but prefer established technology in the digital arena. Others will consider innovation depending on budget, partnerships, or some other factor. (For example, OVG is willing to invest and innovate heavily in sustainability, reflecting their overarching corporate value.) You may find conversations with leaders within your organization productive in determining how your organization should approach innovation and risk. Where and when does your organization want to be on the cutting edge or follow the pack, and why?

YOU'RE ALWAYS GOING SOMEWHERE

I've talked about the importance of understanding the nature of your sport and how the structure and values of your organization might impact your technology choices, especially in the area of innovation. In the next chapter, I guide you in thinking about where your organization is going.

The only way to be effective in a sea of constantly changing technology is to continue to come back to the organization and its business goals. How will a technology help the organization? How will it create efficiency, drive revenue, create fan experience, or reduce risk? How will it support the specific goals that you have and the three-to-five-year vision of where your organization is going? If someone selling you technology can't tell you how they will help you achieve specific business outcomes, show them the door.

CHAPTER ONE: THOUGHT WORK

Before moving on to the next chapter, pull together notes on the following. How does each topic impact how your organization should implement technology?

- the nature of your sport
- the structure of your organization
- your business model and how your organization makes most of its revenue
- organizational values and priorities
- your risk culture and approach to innovation

2

WHERE ARE YOU GOING?

In 2011, NASCAR was facing a turning point. Twelve years earlier, they had signed national TV deals that catapulted the sport to new heights. Suddenly, they had more fans and more money than ever before, as races were broadcast into Americans' living rooms. Then the economic downturn in 2008 crushed the middle-class fans, and they weren't able to come to the same number of races they once had. As John Martin, the CTO at NASCAR, recently described, the situation came to a head when the organization realized they "just had too many licensees . . . not nurturing that sort of connection to the sport." As NASCAR is owned and run by a family who cares intensely about the sport, that didn't sit well with them.

By 2011, NASCAR knew they faced a difficult choice: They could continue to sell digital media rights to third parties as they had been, or they could take their digital technology in-house. Either choice would have financial implications for the sport as a whole. New advances in technology meant that it was possible to engage fans in a way not previously available, but it would be costly. NASCAR didn't have the internal staff to make the transition, so they would need to lean on outside partners at least in the beginning. And they would have to give up the guaranteed income from the digital media rights side of the business.

According to Martin, the decision ultimately came down to who NASCAR was and where they wanted to go. "[We had] the goal of eventually being able to control our own destiny, manage our own resources." They wanted to respect their fans and grow the sport as a whole. Leadership went back and forth, considering the financials carefully, but ultimately, they decided on the path that gave them the most control. Martin told the executive team that if they had the staff internally, they'd be able to engage with fans on the website and via other technologies in ways that would have a much greater impact on the sport.

While every decision in sports technology has business impact, and that business impact should be carefully considered, oftentimes the choice between two paths does come down to the values of the organization. NASCAR sees itself as a sport at the bleeding edge of automotive technology, and it made sense to extend that identity into digital technology as well. But it's also very much an organization focused on common sense and managed risk, so they decided to hire a "technology owner's rep" who could advise them on the process. (That ultimately ended up being our team at OMNIGON, a company I cofounded that's now a part of Next League.)*

* We were heavily involved in the NASCAR project referenced. We sold OMNIGON to a European sports marketing group in 2016 but bought it back in 2024. It's now a part of Next League. So, while the name was different, in a meaningful sense, it's still us.

Taking Victory Laps

Martin recently reflected on the project: "You know, we can look back now and say the decision was correct, right?" The company saw the impact of relationships with its fans and the good revenue and the control of their destiny. It had been a risky but successful decision.

But the journey had also given them a taste for leading with technology: "Each time we had a more successful technology project completion, the company became like, what else can you do?" NASCAR built its own databases, ad operations, and website technologies, among many more technologies, and takes on leading-edge projects in gaming and AR/VR/MR.* They continue to lead with a growing group of dedicated technologists in-house and supplementary support outside: "I call it NASCAR-izing your technology. You can run a pretty lean staff with some really good folks, with that third-party outside support. Do these things on your own . . . in each case with a third-party real expertise in that field to guide us and then eventually let us handle it ourselves."

NASCAR knew they wanted to set the pace for technology adoption in their field, and they've made smart decisions in that direction ever since.

HAVING THE COURAGE TO LOOK AHEAD

There is a dynamic that exists in every company, not just sports organizations. When people do the same job every day, they tend toward the same patterns. They don't have any incentive to revisit processes or technology; they're keeping the trains running on time.

---

* Augmented, virtual, and mixed reality technologies.

The status quo prevails—it feels safe and avoids risk. In technology, the cost of the status quo creates entropy because, left in a static state, technology will begin to fail as the world around it changes.

For many large sports organizations, their businesses have been creating predictable revenue through simple but extremely effective models for years. The combination of national and local media rights deals supported by ticket sales, partnerships, and licensing has driven these large organizations for decades. Asking one of these executives to start investing in innovation or technology because it may shift the dynamics of the business in the future, or because these models may be threatened, is difficult to digest. Often the future feels vague, and the long-term effects of innovation can often not be proven in the short term.

Yet, as seen in the NASCAR story, having the foresight to invest in technology *ahead* of the curve can pay off in concrete ways. As of the time of the story, more and more of their fans were going online. Their business model was going to change sooner or later. Even so, taking the plunge took courage. They made significant financial and time investments without any guarantees of the outcome, but ten years later their vision bears out. The new business model has been successfully proven, and they're now looking forward again.

HARNESSING THE WINDS OF CHANGE

The decisions involving investments in technology are not ones to be made once and forgotten. In fact, there should be a regular reevaluation of both decisions and the downstream impact of those decisions. The strategy around the selection and deployment of technology is a constantly changing, constantly adjusting dance to adapt to the changing world. The key is to embrace that impermanence and make it work in your favor.

Every organization is going somewhere. Either it can be swept along in the winds of change in the larger industry and world, or it can set its own course, tacking its sails to harness the winds of change. The most successful organizations are, in fact, like sailing ships—constantly assessing where they are, where they want to be, and the best way to leverage shifting winds. Technology can significantly improve the journey.

Every organization needs to know where they are going in two senses: First, they must choose their next port of call. Namely, they must create a strategic plan for where they are going and how technology will help, which I will discuss in this chapter. Next, the organization must chart a course between the current state and that port so that they can begin the journey and arrive on time. That is what I'll describe in chapters three and four.

In this chapter, you will be strategic. Like NASCAR, you will determine where you want to go. As circumstances change, you can then compare the direction you are going to that north star. Is your business being driven toward your goals, or are you moving away? Are you making progress on your most important goals? To get there, you must first determine those goals.

CREATING YOUR NORTH STAR

A ship is safe in harbor,
but that's not what ships are for.

—John A. Shedd

A north star is the highest level of goal setting. It answers the question of where your organization is going in the next five to ten years in concrete, measurable, and realistic terms.* What does success look like for you? Without clear answers to these questions, decision-making becomes difficult, and technology investments become much more risky. A north star protects against the instinct to blindly follow short-term revenue. It allows for clear and enduring vision and consistent, productive communication.

In contrast, when organizations don't have a north star, they react to one decision at a time. A passing whim from a leader, the board, or anyone else becomes difficult for people to push back against. Effort becomes wasted on diffuse priorities rather than concentrated on useful results—well-meaning people pull in different directions, causing expensive delays. A north star, on the other hand, empowers *everyone* to remain focused and to translate the big picture into coherent decisions. It makes the next actions clear even in changing circumstances.

EXAMPLES OF NORTH STAR VISIONS

Here are some examples of other organizations making deliberate choices toward their long-term future, and the impact those long-term visions had.

In 1993, Commissioner Gary Bettman proposed that the National Hockey League continue to make a big bet on their future. For the NHL to become one of the biggest leagues in sports, they

---

* While goal setting and execution practices are beyond the scope of this book, I will point out that the difference between *good* goal setting and bad goal setting is immense. If you are not already familiar with OKRs, as well as standard approaches such as SMART goals, I recommend a refresher.

would have to embrace more geographic expansion—a move that at the time appeared both shocking and foolish. Few people played hockey outside of the Midwest, Northeast, and Canada. The league had already recently added the San Jose Sharks, Tampa Bay Lightning, and Ottawa Senators, and in Bettman's first year, they added the Florida Panthers and Mighty Ducks of Anaheim. The idea that more Californians and Floridians would watch a sport on ice was unthinkable. Yet, fast-forward thirty years, and the Florida Panthers were in the Stanley Cup final for the third year in a row, and champions back to back in 2023–24 and 2024–25. The Tampa Bay Lightning have won three Stanley Cups. That didn't happen by accident. In fact, a series of strategic decisions had to be made—and executed—for decades, often with significant financial outlay. The NHL had to have a clear north star.

NASCAR's vision of the future wasn't just about technology but also where their sport as a whole was going. In 2020, NASCAR officially banned the Confederate flag at all events.* In reference to this decision, Tim Clark, NASCAR's executive vice president and chief brand officer, said to me in a recent discussion, "You get to the point where you've really got to stand for something. You have to send a signal that what you think you know about the NASCAR brand or what you may think of NASCAR as a whole is not exactly what you think it is . . . There are people that I think recognize [the ban of the flag] as a really big signal that we are open to everyone, not just the core fans, not just the new fans, but all fans. And no one should feel uncomfortable going to one of our events or being

---

* *ESPN.com*. 2020. "NASCAR Bans Confederate Flags from All Racetracks," June 10, 2020. https://www.espn.com/racing/nascar/story/_/id/29293767/nascar-bans-confederate-flags-racetracks.

associated with our brand . . . [We became] intentional of the things that we stand for and the things that we stand against." NASCAR leadership drew a line in the sand. They began a diversity initiative. Now they have multiple drivers and team owners of color. They decided who they were and made strategic decisions to shape the future of their sport. Clark took a moment to add, "I would be lying if I said that it wasn't also a positive thing for our business." The strategic decision ultimately translated into good business results for them, based on who they were.

For another example, while the PGA TOUR, NASCAR, and others took their digital media rights back in the early 2010s, the NHL did the opposite, selling their digital rights to MLBam in August 2015.* Media rights deals often balance optimizing revenue against distribution and control. In this case, the upside in revenue won. It was a great deal for the NHL, and they were then able to do without the staff they would have needed to manage the technology themselves. Other organizations chose the opposite—you will need to choose the options that make the most sense for your own north star.

A north star can serve as a long-term, directional vision, useful for multiple decades, as MLB's does and as the NHL's geographic expansion did. In other cases, a north star may guide the organization effectively for some period of time and then be revisited.

Who will your organization be in the next ten years, and how can technology impact that vision? What are the opportunities, and

* Soper, Taylor. 2015. "MLB's tech arm preps to spin out into $3B business, inks big rights deal with NHL." *GeekWire*, August 4, 2015. https://www.geekwire.com/2015/mlbs-tech-arm-preps-to-spin-out-into-3b-business-inks-big-rights-deal-with-nhl/.

what's coming next? Circumstances will change, but an organization with a clear vision can adjust with the tides.

Take a moment and write down your own understanding of your organization's north star.

THREE TIME HORIZONS

The north star isn't the only time horizon to consider when approaching your technology. North stars should be clear as to the business goals but leave space for strategic decisions in the meantime.

There are two other time scales critical to sports executives. The medium term is the next three to five years of business outcomes to be delivered. Most sports organizations—and most organizations in the world—buy technology in three-to-five-year purchasing cycles. They invest with large-scale capital expenditure (CapEx) budgets, often millions of dollars. Then they operate the technology out of an operations budget (OpEx), increasing budget as technology maintenance needs build over time. Eventually the company priorities change and/or the technology needs to be updated, and it invests in a new CapEx technology build to last another three to five years. The majority of the critical decisions in technology happen in the context of this cycle.

The last, and most important, time scale in sports technology is the next twelve to eighteen months. Most technology leaders have yearly roadmaps, and the daily work of planning and implementing the technology—as well as maintaining!—happens at this scale. This time scale rightly takes up a huge amount of mental space for technology leaders. Failing to get the next twelve months correct *will* lead to failed implementations and limited job security.

CHARTING YOUR NEXT THREE TO FIVE YEARS

Now that you know your north star, consider where the organization is going in the medium term. What is the direction over the next three to five years? What is next for technology, and where should the technology group be in that time period? What capital investments should be made?

Then, once you know the three-to-five-year vision for the technology group, turn that vision into intermediate *outcomes* or milestones over the next year or two. Stay high level; you'll return to this list in the next chapter as you consider your immediate roadmap. Right now, it's time to do the preparatory thinking.

STRATEGY GETS YOU FUNDING

Despite the many pressures to focus solely on the next twelve to twenty-four months as a technology leader, I strongly recommend thinking more broadly. Technologists should regularly review all three time horizons. They should know their north star and understand where the business is going. They keep the trains running on time. *And* they do the mid-level strategic work, connecting the two. Thinking strategically about what technology needs to accomplish creates opportunities for your organization. It also helps you do your job better.

Understanding where you are going allows you to make compelling business cases for decisions. A multi-million dollar spend for technology is, by itself, a heavy lift. If you can connect that investment back to a critical initiative, that same budget is far more likely to be approved. (You may also be able to get additional funds by adding strategic partnerships for additional revenue; see later in the chapter.)

Doing the strategic work means you can point to the rationale for the decisions you're making. You earn trust from the executives around you and the board, and you earn the right to attempt larger risks. Strategy makes you more effective at your job and more valuable to the organization.

The Courage to Address Gaps

All too often, technology professionals think it's a sign of weakness to admit that they are not good at something. In fact, self-awareness is by far the biggest strength any executive can have. A weakness that's identified is one that can be addressed and compensated for. But if someone ignores that weakness, the gap will remain, and will undermine progress, forever. All of us have limitations; the difference is how we approach them.

Many technologists come up through an organization by learning how to solve complex problems and deliver technology. They can build whatever anyone asks of them. Learning to think strategically, and to connect technology back to critically important business decisions, can feel like a stretch. If you're a smart, technically oriented executive with an engineering background, take stock of your strategic skills. Have the intellectual humility and openness to ask your people about them. Then, if you need to skill up or hire someone to help you think through the three-to-five-year time horizon, do so. The same goes for any technical skill gap you may have—it's far better to address that gap or hire for it than to let it continue indefinitely.

Now that you have a clear idea of the three time horizons and the direction of your business in the near term, I'll walk you through the additional thinking you'll need to do before concrete delivery planning begins. Make note of your risk culture and its impact on pacing and delivery, your budget, revenue opportunities, and priorities. Then, make note of the extra space that you'll need to leave in your schedule as you begin planning, in the next chapter.

YOUR RISK PROFILE SETS THE PACE

If your north star and three-to-five-year business outcomes set the direction, your risk culture will set how quickly your organization can move.

Consider the risk culture that your organization has built, as shown by their attitude toward innovation. If your company is willing to tolerate risk and loss, you will be able to move more quickly and take bigger bets for potential rewards. If your company is more traditional and risk averse, you will have to move more slowly and in discrete stages on the way to bigger goals.

That being said, as my partner, and Next League's CTO, Mike Grushin says, "technology is best built in iterations." Trying to build the tech version of the Taj Mahal all at once is too risky for nearly any organization. Instead, manage risk by rolling out technology in stages. Each stage can go live before specific dates, and the organization gets value from each release. Plan for more lower-risk stages for a more risk-averse organization.

Iteration is a good risk management approach because it also allows for adjustment. As the world changes, the team can choose to adapt the technology to a slightly different version of itself or even to pivot to something else entirely.

How quickly can you move within your organization? How much proof do you have to show? How can you plan within your time and budget limitations to show results at the pace your organization prefers? Stay high level but take notes as to how this aspect of your organization impacts planning.

DETERMINE YOUR BUDGET

There are two viable approaches to determining a technology budget. The first and most common is being assigned a number by the business and then determining what technology fits within that budget. That approach leads to prioritization stress. Alternatively, you can consider what technology the organization will need and then translate that technology into a cost number. That approach leads to stress from price, since most organizations don't know exactly what features and technology they truly need.

Here are some questions that help when considering your budget for technology at a high level:

- What do we need to build?
- How much does it cost to build those things?
- What can we afford for the budget we have?
- How much of the budget could be offset by new revenue that results from what is built?

Make a note of what you roughly have to spend, for you to return to in the next chapter with the prioritization and feature exercises. If your fixed budget or available funds are smaller than your needed budget (which it nearly always is), you'll need to find business partnerships to pay for the difference. (See discussion below.)

Even with partnership deals, however, you will still have to make hard decisions in terms of time. No one can fit ten pounds of sugar in a five-pound bag. The strategic work is assessing the size of the bag and the sugar that will fit into it.

LEAVE ROOM FOR THE UNKNOWN

Because every sports organization will deal with many last-minute changes over a year, I recommend leaving 20 to 25 percent of your planned effort open. (If you can put 40 percent aside, do that, but for most organizations, that is not realistic.) Opportunities and challenges will arise that cannot be foreseen, and having space for them makes execution easier.

For similar reasons, I also recommend spending only 75 to 80 percent of your planned CapEx budget on known technology builds. (This number should include the buffer that a good project manager will put into the system for unknown expenditures.) Then, plan on spending that additional 20 to 25 percent this year, and next year for a smaller CapEx budget, on things that you cannot foresee.

Leaving room for the unexpected prevents major budget issues in your future.

FINDING ADDITIONAL REVENUE

Fortunately, budget is not entirely dependent on the resources of a given organization. As I'll cover in more depth in the partnerships and advertising chapter, many technologies can be attached to partners to acquire additional funding.

As of the time of this writing, the biggest companies in the world care intensely about sports, and I expect this will remain true when you read this. The NFL is by far the largest sports organization by annual revenue, which topped $23 billion in 2024, and it is dwarfed by the size of companies like Apple ($391 billion in 2024[*]), Amazon ($638 billion in 2024[†]) and Google ($350 billion in 2024[‡]). The money is there, and companies are interested in partnering with sports organizations because they love our fans.

The biggest companies in the world love sports fans because fans are intensely loyal. The longevity and loyalty of the fans are what drive the longevity of this business. The fans are the single greatest asset of any sports organization and why sports organizations *must* take the long view.

THINK IN OUTCOMES

In my other book, *Zero Sales: Generating Services Revenue Without Selling*, I discuss the difference between someone seeking a predefined solution and someone looking for a business outcome. I cannot tell you how often I hear of a sports organization putting out an RFP for a new website, for example, without any clear idea of what that website might deliver for the business that is different from the current website.[§] In one recent case, I saw a sales department asking about what new assets they'd have as part of the new website when

* finance.yahoo.com/news/apple-stock-hits-all-time-high-market-cap-touches-4-trillion-as-iphone-momentum-tech-rally-boosts-shares-133959746.html

† aboutamazon.com/news/company-news/amazon-ceo-andy-jassy-2024-letter-to-shareholders

‡ abc.xyz/investor/events/event-details/2025/2024-Q4-Earnings-Call

§ Personally, I would argue that RFPs are normally counterproductive for most sports organizations. The only way that you can effectively issue an RFP is to have predefined exactly the solution you need and ask builders of that solution to execute your orders. Sports organizations need, instead, to work with experienced partners who can provide several paths to a given outcome and help them find the one that has the most impact for the least total spend.

in fact no one purchasing the website thought to include new assets at all. The new website cost millions of dollars and delivered no new value to the business until that new inventory was added at additional cost and time.

"Build a website" is a task—a large task, a project-level task—but not one that has any sense of outcomes attached. If, on the other hand, you take the time to define the business *outcome* you want with good measurements—such as $X new revenue from that website—you are far more likely to achieve useful business results. Good metrics also allow for easy pivots if the first attempt doesn't provide enough results to meet the outcome.

Determine where you are going as an organization, then find the outcomes—not tasks—that get you there for the best results.

MAKING MEANINGFUL PROGRESS

Occasionally I will have a conversation with an executive who feels reluctant to do long-term planning because they feel circumstances will inevitably change. Certainly leadership can shift and goals change, and no one can possibly anticipate everything when building out a roadmap beyond a single year. If a partner is excited to spend millions of dollars to promote specific technology as part of a broader relationship, it may not be on the roadmap, but the sales team will push it and the technology team will build it.

In those moments, you will have to take the attitude of a sailing ship. When the winds change, you must adjust your sails so that you continue to travel in the direction of your next port. Sometimes leadership will look at an opportunity, decide that it's not who you are as an organization, and say no. Other times, in an effort to acquire the revenue, and assuming you have time and budget free, the impact of that will be lessened. Regardless, the change is inevitable. Life in sports technology is a long-distance journey.

Of course, no one makes it to a sailing destination port without a careful plan and good charts. Good planning is not optional in our business and reaching your goal means making smart decisions—in advance—for the next twelve to eighteen months.

Let's get started.

CHAPTER TWO: THOUGHT WORK

Before moving on to the next chapter, pull together the following thought work from this chapter. You can always read through the book once and return to the action work on a second read if needed.

- **your north star,** or long-term (five-to-ten-year) vision
- your medium-term (three-to-five-year) **list of business outcomes** desirable to achieve with technology
- **notes on your risk culture** and any limitations it may impose in terms of technology and innovation you can deploy
- **your CapEx and OpEx budgets,** minus buffer for existing commitments and 20 to 25 percent held back effort and expenditures
- notes on how to create additional **partnership revenue** and an estimate of what could be added to CapEx, if applicable
- **any hard dates that cannot be moved** and hard timeline requirements for the business

3

OUTCOMES AND CHOOSING TECHNOLOGY

Remember Perkins Miller from the last chapter, the executive with experience at WWE, the NFL, and the Olympics? He is, in his words, a "get what you plan for kind of guy." He's thrived in situations with no tolerance for missing deadlines, and he says the only way to succeed in that environment is to plan. The more innovative the technology the organization wants, the more intense the planning must be to manage the risk of *new*.

Sports technology also has specific challenges. We must hit delivery windows that cannot move. The technology often needs to be "something that is going to scale across multiple platforms, from your PC to your mobile phone, your tablet or your gaming console or TV app," as Miller says. The content must be delivered faithfully regardless of medium, often with little or no latency. Video especially can make scaled delivery challenging due to bandwidth and entitlement requirements. You've got to serve "consumer tech data with a lot of stability built in because you've got to scale it," often to millions of people at once.

To be clear, delivering scalable technology is difficult, much less within budget and in relation to a date that cannot move. These kinds of projects can go very, very wrong. In 2013, the initial launch of the Healthcare.gov website failed miserably as five times as much traffic as anticipated hit the site, causing it to crash. Although the issues were eventually corrected, the $94 million budget ballooned to $1.7 *billion*. Over the past ten years, 94 percent of enterprise federal information technology projects were unsuccessful, more than 50 percent were delayed *and* over budget, and over 40 percent were determined to be complete failures. Federal IT projects have dates that can and do move, and they regularly fail anyway. Our industry can't afford that kind of failure rate.

Sports executives must keep a close eye on the moving parts. Miller has a history of meticulousness in every detail of a build and bringing technology projects in on time and on budget. To do that, he says planning is absolutely critical; he credits much of his success to a robust process that includes "back planning and strategy work and *then* execution . . . When something's got to be done, it's got to be done right. Or you won't make that deadline."

I couldn't agree more, which is why we're talking about planning and how to do it well in the next two chapters.

WHY WE PLAN

Failing to plan is planning to fail.

—Benjamin Franklin

Because timelines and costs are inflexible in sports, it's critical to do detailed tactical planning *before* implementing technology. A rigorous plan keeps risk down. But planning once and then executing isn't sufficient either—sports organizations and their technology partners must be constantly checking in, adjusting to the situation as it evolves. They must manage the change that surrounds the technology at all times.

Once a captain sets the destination for a ship, he will chart the course. He does this so that there's a plan that can be followed and shared with others. Everyone understands that plan in case there are issues along the way. The ship will set sail, and the captain will constantly check its position against the tides and winds, asking the crew to adjust the sails as they go. Technology works in the same way. If you have no destination in mind, how are you going to get there? How do you chart a course to nowhere?

> *If you don't know where you are going, you might wind up someplace else.*
>
> **—Yogi Berra**

If you do know where you're going but can't adjust to changes in tides and winds, you won't make it to your destination. Every technology project with any scale will have failures and/or adjustments that must be made during the journey. The question is, What will you do when one occurs?

THE COMPETENCIES MODEL

I believe there are four essential competencies required inside all technology units that must exist for any project to be delivered on time and within budget:

- **Counsel**—experienced technology practitioners who can provide thousand-foot-view decisions based on business outcomes and technical knowledge
- **Choice**—the decisions on which specific technologies to use and how, and who will build them, whether internally or externally
- **Governance**—the decision of who's responsible for what, who owns the outcome, and the process and/or design that will be used
- **Execution**—the day-to-day delivery decisions encapsulated in code and built technology; normally includes clear measurement of results and adjustment if those measurements don't land along the way

While each competency is dependent on the others, there are generally ordered steps to approach these competencies in any project.

THE STEPS

To deliver on time and within budget, I recommend doing the following for each technology program and project:

1. **Roadmap your desired business outcomes** and how you will measure and monitor those outcomes.
2. **Analyze and choose technology products** required to achieve those outcomes.
3. **Decide on using in-house or external partners.**
4. **Sell the project internally,** beginning the hiring or partner evaluation after getting the internal go-ahead.

5. **Develop a project plan,** backing out of the date that will not move, highlighting dependencies, and specifying what milestones are and when they will be achieved.
6. **Implement the technology,** designing, building, and deploying it effectively.
7. **Measure and monitor the result** and adjust regularly, as needed.

I'll cover steps 1 and 2 in this chapter and steps 3 through 7 in the next chapter. Keep in mind that some steps will require more effort than others, and the entirety of the process can be lengthy. The plan will also evolve, as you constantly check it against changing circumstances, and update as you go.

As a note, steps 2 and 3 can be done in either order. If your organization has the internal capability to analyze products so that you can get 80 percent of the features for 50 percent of the price, use the order I've outlined. If your organization needs or wants help to select the absolute best technology product or needs help with setting up the process as outlined in this chapter, do step 3 (selecting an outside partner, the next chapter) first, as they will help with technology selection.

Step 1: Roadmap Your Desired Business Outcomes

Before planning or executing, you'll need to collect the following information from the last chapter, if you have not already. Feel free to read through the book once for a high-level overview and return to this chapter and the next again when you're ready to execute.

Here are the planning preparation materials you'll need:

- **your north star,** or longer-term (five-to-ten-year) vision for the business, or at least your area of the business
- your medium-term (three-to-five-year) **list of business outcomes** desirable to achieve with technology
- **notes on your risk culture,** and any limitations it may impose in terms of technology and innovation you can deploy
- **your CapEx and OpEx budgets,** minus buffer for held-back effort and expenditures
- notes on how to create additional **partnership revenue** and estimate of what could be added to CapEx, if applicable
- **any hard dates that cannot be moved** and hard timeline requirements for the business

For the remainder of this chapter and the next, I'll assume you know your budget, timelines, and desired outcomes.

Choosing Near-Term Outcomes

Most organizations have a sense of the upcoming technology projects that they will tackle over the next twelve to eighteen months. This sense is rarely perfectly correlated with their actual capacity, by the way—I have never seen a circumstance in which the plan for upcoming technology projects did not exceed the resources available for it. Yet, despite them having a sense of what's coming, many sports organization technology groups will struggle with translating strategy into a concrete roadmap. In fact, we've had to counsel many of our clients with the specific skills involved.

Start in this preparation step by choosing the specific *outcomes* that you will tackle for the next twelve to eighteen months.

1. **Choose the outcomes that should happen *first*** to serve the business's three- to five-year goals. If a foundational technology is required to deliver the desired outcome you have targeted for five years from now, that investment may need to be made now. The design, build, deployment, and optimization of enterprise technologies is usually a multiyear endeavor.
2. **Consider which outcomes provide the most benefit** (revenue, fan engagement, or lowered risk, for example) in comparison with their cost, if you have a clear idea of each. Prioritize those first.

Then, create a formal roadmap.

Building a Roadmap

Most engineers responsible for planning have a roadmap in the form of a spreadsheet, or a software platform like Notion, or Miro—this is often a loosely ordered list of technical tasks for the near term, with specifications and personnel attached. Over time, as business needs change and their boss has new requests, a good engineer will reorder the list some. But the result rarely reflects higher-order strategic thinking. This is not what I mean by a roadmap.

A well-planned technology roadmap is a highly strategic document. It maps out the project steps needed on the way to the business outcomes, and the map changes as priorities change. My team creates a separate project plan document and tracking system for each project, which we'll discuss below. We keep the to-do list off the main priorities roadmap, but you can also add them to your strategic roadmap in detail if your team is small.

There are extensive resources available both online and in book form on how to translate strategy and milestones into an effective roadmap. That being said, building a strategic roadmap is a practical skill that cannot be completely learned from writing. I strongly recommend making sure that you are working with someone (inside or outside of your team) with experience creating and executing strategic roadmaps at a high level. Without this part of the work being done well, you may end up in a situation where your tech stack has to be pulled apart and rebuilt to function. Competent **counsel** in this area could save you immense cost.

While keeping in mind the need for hands-on counsel, I will provide some general guidance below.

Consider Commitments and Watch Capacity

As you translate your outcomes into technology milestones for your team to deliver against, consider your existing commitments as a technology organization. What upcoming requests and technologies have already been agreed to? How much time does your team need to keep the business operating properly? How much technical debt will you have to work down over the course of the next eighteen months? All these questions will need to be considered alongside your new goals.

One hundred percent of organizations wind up scheduling in excess of their capacity—and one hundred percent of organizations fail to deliver beyond their capacity. If you plan for this reality, you will become one of the best planners in sports technology. So, right now, take one final gut check, considering your project list and commitments in light of your capacity. Cut anything that you can cut and leave 20 to 25 percent of your planned time for the unexpected demands of the year, more if your organization is prone to last-minute changes. If you have outcomes or projects left over, consider whether you will hire or outsource to cover the additional work or whether you will extend timelines. Your budget and your organization's values should guide decisions.

The Roadmap Will Change

No matter how well you plan, there will always be more things on the roadmap than there are hours in the year. The sales team and executive teams will arrive with new opportunities. Reality will arrive with new challenges. To stay on any kind of useful schedule, then, you will need to prioritize, reprioritize, and (possibly) outsource—and then prioritize, reprioritize, and outsource again. A true roadmap is closely aligned with the priorities of the organization at any given moment, and since those priorities change, so must the roadmap.

I have had conversations with sports executives who expressed irritation about the technology or features their teams have released, because the executive forgot why it was in the pipeline to begin with, or the rationale was never clear. Don't let this happen to you; keep your roadmap up to date as a repository of your strategic prioritization work and accept that the updating and reprioritizing may never end.

Make Responsibilities Clear

The governance of a project, who is responsible for that project, who makes decisions related to it, and who ultimately owns the outcome, is a critical determination of successful projects. An executive's job is to deliver the outcomes needed for the business, and that includes creating and defining roles for people working for them. My experience is that the most success comes when everyone clearly understands each role's responsibility and KPIs.* How will success be measured? On what outcomes will the person be judged and by when? Ensure the entire team knows exactly where they fit within the scope of the project or program. When you give people clear expectations and attainable outcomes, they will focus and perform at their best. Then, it becomes a matter of meeting together regularly to spot issues or gaps.

Next League has hired quite a few people lately, and we spend a great deal of time setting expectations. We create thirty-, sixty-, and ninety-day plans, with the outcomes they are expected to achieve this year and the measurements of those achievements if they are successful. Then, we back out of the year and talk about quarterly and monthly goals. Only at that point do we help them create any task lists. Once someone knows that if they accomplish these, say, five things, they are successful, they tend to rise to the occasion. We do similar work when a new project is spun up, clearly defining who needs to accomplish what and by when.

As a note, software developers also talk about governance in terms of the controls placed on any given system. For example, who is allowed to push code, and how? I consider this a subset of overall governance, as it should follow naturally from who is responsible for which outcomes.

Take a moment and assign responsibility for each outcome on your roadmap to a specific person.

---

* Key performance indicators, or the metrics against the person's work, will be judged.

Measuring and Monitoring Outcomes

Each outcome should have concrete KPIs or metrics attached to it, which you will measure and monitor as you execute the plan. If there is a gap, or progress is less than expected, having these KPIs in place allows you to make meaningful adjustments in time to course-correct.

To give an example of measurements, a desired business outcome might be increasing ticket sales by a certain revenue number (the KPI). There can be many possible paths to increasing ticket sales, including (1) increasing landing page traffic by 20 percent, (2) adding visible buy buttons to certain digital properties, or (3) doing an analysis of the existing user journey to ticket sales, with an eye to making it far easier to buy a ticket. In fact, doing more of all these activities might increase ticketing revenue. When determining your roadmap, plan out which path or paths you will take and who is responsible for them. However, measure your KPIs steadily to see the impact of your efforts and don't be afraid to diversify or pivot your efforts to other, better paths as you go.

Step 2: Choose Your Technology Investments

- making your strategy actionable
- needs analysis
- gap analysis
- cost-benefit analysis

In this step, you will choose the types of technology investments required to deliver your outcomes, if you have not already done so. Then, you will analyze technology products and choose brands whose features and capabilities match your budget and needs.

Making Your Strategy Actionable

Begin with the business outcomes your technology should deliver over the next twelve to eighteen months. Use the information in part two of the book to help you connect strategy to *types* of technology.

Let's go through a simple example to illustrate how this is done. The Fictitious Sports Association (FSA) is planning the next eighteen months. While their sport has a pro league, it does not yet have a critical mass of fans. (There are not tens of millions of people watching them on TV yet.) So a logical business objective for the association is to grow the sport as a whole. The path to their desired future will include—but not be limited to—technology.

The first priority for the FSA in terms of technology is data. They want to find people who care about their sport and talk to them, with the eventual goal of increasing the numbers of fans and monetizing them. Once they know their immediate need—building a data asset—they can identify general technology types and then attach technology requirements to that need.

Needs Analysis

Once the immediate-term business goals are known, the needs analysis is straightforward, if thinking-heavy. How do the goals translate into the specific things the organization will need to reach those goals? Make sure that you identify *every* item or technology that your organization will need to reach its goals.

For the FSA, they will need a way to collect data, a way to store and segment that data, and several specific features that will allow their sales and marketing teams to use that data strategically. After research, the association finds they need a CRM, with data collection and marketing technology features that may or may not belong to a separate marketing or data solution.

The association makes a list of each feature it will need and the technology *types* (like the CRM or marketing list management technology) that they will likely need to buy. Since they're a new association with little existing technology, they will do a quick check of their existing contracts and commitments rather than a full gap analysis.

For a different example, the established Large Sports League (LSL) wants to launch a direct-to-consumer product with the goal of producing revenue directly from fans. The league decides to deliver their product through their existing app and as part of their web platform, which will both need more functionality than they currently have.

The LSL will have *some* but not all of the building blocks for this product already. Their web platform doesn't have identity management because they serve content to everyone equally and there's nothing that is user specific. They may already have the technologies required to stream live games or the CRM to keep track of who has already purchased. To avoid wasting money, the league will need to go through a full and rigorous needs and gap analysis process to assess what tech they have that can be used and what will need to be procured and integrated.

To properly go through the needs analysis process, you and your team must translate each of your business outcomes into the technology required to deliver those outcomes. Most sports executives leverage counsel and/or technical experts in specific areas of technology to make these decisions. Consider reading through part two of this book to help.

Applying Strategy to Needs Decisions

When considering more than one path to the same outcome, apply the north star and medium-term strategy to help set your direction. Then, consider the speed at which your outcomes can move and your organization's tolerance for risk and innovation. Would a tried-and-true approach be more appropriate for a specific outcome, or would an innovative approach provide more brand lift? If a technology can only be invested in if it's funded through a partnership, this has timeline implications that should also be considered as part of your needs. (Sometimes the sales team must sell the partnership and secure the revenue before it can be allocated to technology; see chapter six.)

While budget considerations come into play during the cost-benefit analysis later, time considerations impact this work now. If you know that a given technology is more complex than you have time to implement, you may choose another path or introduce an iterative release schedule. You must also consider dependencies. For example, if technology A must be fully implemented before technology B, and B has a hard deadline, you will need to consider if implementing both is feasible in the time you have.

Create a Comparison List

Before moving on to the gap analysis step, create a list of technology needs by feature and product category. Divide your list into "must have," "nice to have," and "may need in the future" items to make comparison easier in subsequent steps. If the technology is likely to lead to greater efficiency or bring in revenue, for example, note that information for use in your cost-benefit analysis later.

If you get stuck on this step, you may wish to hire an outside provider with expertise in sports technology to help you assess and choose technologies. Skip ahead to step 3. [Side note, I often use the term *provider* not *vendor* intentionally. In the complex world of sports technology, you need companies that are willing to approach your needs with a flexible, solutions-oriented offering—this is what technology services providers do. Vendors sell finished products or services directly to consumers or businesses.]

Gap Analysis

- Assess your organization's existing technology and abilities.
- Consider your technical documentation and debt and decide how that impacts what you can use.
- Identify the gaps between what you have and what you will need.

If the needs analysis identifies what your organization needs to reach its goals, the gap analysis identifies what your organization needs, but does not already have.

A gap analysis is simple in theory: The organization should take its list of needs, compare it to technology categories it already has, and then identify what investment will be required to fill the gap. For older organizations, though, identifying what you have (and can use!) can be complex.

Begin with a detailed top-down audit of what technologies you already have.* The inventory should not be limited to the presence or absence of a technology—look deeper to make sure that it delivers what is needed. For example, the established sports league from earlier in the chapter needs a content management system, but the one they have is missing important functionality.

Technical Debt and Documentation Assessment

Next, consider the present state of each technology and whether it can be used as is or needs to be modified—or replaced. A simple *green*, *yellow*, or *red* code may be helpful to represent each decision. Apply *green* if you will definitely use that technology, even if it must be modified. Use *yellow* if the answer will depend on the final budget reality or the level of modification needed. *Yellow* technologies can be replaced if there is sufficient budget or made to work if there is not. To do this exercise correctly, you'll need to consider your technical and documentation debt at length.

Where Technical Debt Comes From

Technical debt usually represents the accumulated problems over years and is a human issue, not a technical one. Due to time and budget constraints, sports technology teams tend to deploy technology in the way that is most practical to achieve the short-term priority and deliver the technology on time. They almost always intend to revisit and use shortcuts or "Band-Aids" in order to make the launch or release date—but they often never get back to it. It's not

* If your organization is less than two years old, like the Fictitious Sports Association, your audit may be abbreviated. Still check to ensure that you understand what technologies are currently being used and paid for.

because they are irresponsible or unfocused but because requests for their time and focus almost never end. They may make minor enhancements but continue to maintain an old technology rather than update or replace it entirely due to time, risk, and cost. Time, because they don't have it. Risk, because often older technology works and has a team that understands it. And cost, because replacing legacy technologies is expensive and time consuming. Technologists in most organizations are judged on the systems not going down and on delivering what is asked: the new form sending an email, a login and password added to a section never intended to support it, layers of taped-on solutions, each requested within unreasonable timeframes.

Over years, the sprawl of jerry-rigged solutions adds up. No one intended to create something brittle that would take down an entire system if not properly managed. No one deliberately built a tangle of taped-on solutions, the proper maintenance of which only lives in the heads of the human beings who developed it (many of whom may be gone). The work was done the way the business allowed it to be done when it was requested. There may be a plan to revisit the technology to make the solution maintainable and sustainable, but there was never enough time to think it through appropriately or to write down what had been done. Instead, they focused on keeping the systems up and doing what was asked.

The problem is that these work patterns become unsustainable. The older systems become clunkier and less stable over time. Making changes becomes dependent on one or two specific people to personally institute the change because only the people who designed the shortcut, know how to fix it. The drip, drip, drip of technical debt adds up. When someone leaves, or the system hits

its breaking point, the debt suddenly becomes due. If Bob is the only one who can update application code, and he gets hit by a bus, suddenly nothing can change in the system without risking breaking it completely.

You can address your technical debt as part of your roadmap, or you risk it coming due all at once, catastrophically, at the worst possible time.

What technical documentation and debt exist in the technology that you currently have? How does it affect what you can and cannot use toward the outcomes you must deliver? Take an honest assessment and revisit your red/yellow/green ratings.

Finishing Your Gap Analysis

At the end of your gap analysis, you should have identified which of your needed features and technologies your organization already has in usable form. Now, compare your needs analysis with what you have. Which technologies can be modified or fixed from what you have, more cheaply? Which technologies and features remain?

You will now have a shortened list of technologies and features to buy.

The Cost-Benefit Analysis and the Choice

Choosing the technology products and platforms for your organization is extremely complicated; there are a *lot* of tools available.

Our team likes to back into choices by comparing the features of each product and commercial terms, in a grid. That approach allows for a side-by-side product comparison. Commercial terms must be a part of that comparison or you are not taking a truly objective view of the choices you need to make. When we are hired to do this work, we refer to it as "bake-offs" and we seek scenarios that deliver 80 to 90 percent of the required functionality for 50 percent of the price.*

Products differentiate themselves on purpose. For example, Salesforce and HubSpot take up the same category, but they work in fundamentally different ways, with different feature sets. Although established enterprise products can be far more expensive, deploying them is often leveraging a Swiss Army knife rather than a scalpel. Since the FSA needs only a single, specific tool, they should likely buy the cheaper option, but only after first examining their twelve-month roadmap.

In our bake-offs we create a matrix with easy-to-understand feature lists and commercial terms. If all the client's boxes are checked with a product that's cheaper, then we normally recommend the client buy the cheaper product. That said, if their roadmap is taking them into a space where they will need a more robust solution later, it often doesn't make sense to save short-term money to incur long-term switching costs. Going through the process of a formal cost-benefit analysis, along with math, is still helpful. I've seen cases where the transition costs later were minimally painful and expensive, and the savings over the next two years far outweighed that cost. I've also seen the reverse.

Take note of potential benefits of each technology, such as increased efficiency or revenue, to help your decision-making.

---

* Credit to Next League advisor Doug Perlman for this phrase.

How to Choose

- Partner products first. (If someone is providing partner funds, they rise to the top of the list.)
- Prioritize well-established enterprise technologies with good support, unless you have a good reason not to.
- Consider initial cost and ongoing costs ("total cost of ownership").
- Maximize flexibility and modularity.

Partner Products First

As we are in the sports technology field, the first and most important criterion for selecting a technology is whether or not the provider/vendor is a partner for the organization. If Microsoft, Google, or Salesforce has contracted for partnership or advertising with the organization, that company's technology is usually the top priority—if it can be made to work for your needs.

Prioritize Well-Established Enterprise Technologies

When in doubt, choose well-established, enterprise-level technologies for your foundational technologies. There are a few reasons for this guideline. Sporting events regularly put technology under extreme loads in very narrow windows; even mature, established technology can struggle at scale, and smaller or startup products may or may not be able to cope even with modification. Enterprise products are often simply lower risk, more tested, and more able to support our edge cases. They also normally come with more formal support processes (often 24/7 support) if an issue arises, which matters in a world where most of the money we make comes from a four-hour window.

That said, sometimes the most important innovation comes from newer and technically less mature businesses. These products will often come with a lower price of functionality that you can't ignore as an important part of your overall strategy. A good rule of thumb is to deploy newer and less mature technology outside of mission-critical launches or releases or after you've seen other sports organizations successfully roll out that technology.

Consider Initial and Total Cost

While price is not the only consideration, it's critically important. Consider compromising on some or all of your "nice to have" features in exchange for a more reasonable price point. Your "bake-off" list will provide a useful metric to compare features between products directly and to compare products and prices more easily.

However, the initial price isn't the only consideration. You may not want to buy the smaller, less-featured product if your three-to-five-year growth means that you will need more features in the future than you do today. You also may—if the cost of migrating to a new product is reasonable and the price difference is enough—do a formal cost-benefit analysis, with math, to determine the right path.

Your cost-benefit math, by the way, should also include the ongoing maintenance or OpEx costs in addition to your CapEx costs. If your team will spend all its time next year tending to a system's maintenance or technical debt, that system is far more costly than a simple CapEx price tag would reflect. Add in estimated operational costs before making your decision, seeking out technical specialists to help with this math if needed.

Flexible and Modular Are Best

As you make decisions about how to choose and implement your technology, I recommend maximizing flexibility and modularity. That way, when your organization's needs change, you can replace a section of your architecture without having to tear all of it out. With proper configuration, you can turn off one feature or section when an issue inevitably arises without affecting the fan's experience on the rest of the system, which buys you both time and goodwill. The demands of our industry make these decisions more important and higher stakes.

RIGOROUS PLANNING CONTROLS RISK

Technology is becoming mission critical to sports organizations, and the decisions of which technologies to use and whether to outsource are highly strategic. Having a clear idea of your organization's capabilities and existing technology allows you to supplement what you have with what you need and make better decisions.

Now that you know what technologies you will be using, and who will implement them, let's turn to the roadmap, the project plan, and implementation. Hitting dates that cannot move is difficult, and to do it, you must handle resourcing, monitoring, and rigorous planning carefully. The process gives you predictable results in terms of time and money when done well. When done badly, the complexity spirals out of control, and the outcomes you want are at risk.

CHAPTER THREE: ACTION LIST

In this chapter, I described how to choose business *outcomes* rather than tasks, create a roadmap, and choose technology strategically. Now, do the legwork to create the following:

- **Counsel.** Involve experienced technology professionals, either internal or external, in creating a rigorous roadmap and establishing a needs analysis and gap analysis. Your *outcomes* should drive your informed decisions.
- **Choice.** Be strategic in selecting technologies that fill the gap between where you are and where you are going. Prioritize partners, established enterprise-level technologies, modular and flexible options, and products with reasonable total costs of ownership.
- **Governance.** Make responsibilities clear. Who is responsible for what project and outcome must be established clearly, along with the metrics by which they will be judged.
- **Execution.** To ensure your execution goes smoothly, account for the existing commitments of your team and your real capacity. Prioritize ruthlessly and cut what you can. Then, add at least 20 to 25 percent additional time to account for the unexpected.

4

DETAILS, PLAN, AND EXECUTION

Last weekend I installed shelves in my basement to organize the space and get boxes off the floor. The directions from the manufacturer were pictures with no words, with many of the steps left to my interpretation. Two of the pieces looked extraordinarily similar, so I found at the end of the project that I had used the wrong one. I had also done a step out of order in assembly, assuming I knew what I was doing. The result was that the shelves worked, but they wouldn't sit flush against the wall, and one side tilted slightly higher than the other. I could tell at a glance I'd done it wrong, but that day I had to be somewhere, so I left it.

When I went back to the basement the next day, I now had two bad options: Was I going to invest more time and effort to disassemble and then reassemble the shelves? Or was I going to leave them wrong? Personally, I hate half-assed work, so I retraced the steps and fixed the problem. But I'd spent literally three times as long as it should have taken to install them in the first place.

Developing and deploying software can be like my shelving project, one more complex than my example. If someone skips steps, does them out of order, or applies a slightly wrong piece, the result—just like with my shelves—may still function. The result may not be visibly wrong, but the mistakes are still there, in the form of technical debt. The piper must be paid. Either the technology group stops work to go back and fix the issue now, or they do so in the future when a problem crops up without warning. In some cases, the resource cost of fixing the issue will be many times greater than having done it correctly in the first place.

THE SEQUENCE AND PROCESS MATTER

Software development needs to follow a process and often be built in a specific order to function well. Doing steps out of order can be catastrophic to the final timeline, product, or both—just like building a piece of furniture. When I assembled shelves in the wrong order, I needed to take them apart and reassemble, at the cost of a few hours. With software, a product that takes literal man-years to create with a team of people, the rework problem can be massive and threaten the project as a whole.

In the last chapter, I discussed the choice of technology, but choice is not enough on its own. To be successful, the project or product manager must also have the counsel, governance, and execution to turn the plan into reality.

Insist on a Detailed Plan

I find the great thing in this world is not so much where we stand, as in what direction we are moving:

To reach the port of heaven, we must sail sometimes with the wind and sometimes against it—but we must sail, and not drift, nor lie at anchor.

—Oliver Wendell Holmes, Sr.

Every now and then I have a conversation with a client who is working on a technology project that doesn't involve our team. When I ask them basic questions about the other company's project planning, the client often says they haven't seen those documents yet. I tell them to insist. Any competent company will be able to show their project plans and progress, and without that work, the entire project becomes incredibly risky. At that point, you're just hoping the project will come in on time and on budget and "hope" doesn't have a great track record.

As I've said before, when a project fails, 99 percent of the time, it's not the fault of the technology. It's a people or a process problem. Don't misunderstand: Choosing the right technology is important—you want the right capabilities for the right cost. But without good people and process, the best technology in the world will fail, as the media company discovered in the story in the introduction. In contrast, I've personally seen great talent implement mediocre technology with a rigorous process and still produce great results. Planning and process are under your control, and planning and process (with regular check-ins) are what will ultimately bring you the predictable results—and lower risk—this job requires.

Ensure you work with a competent project manager or managers, yourself or others, so that someone is clearly in charge. But also, be absolutely certain that you plan for success.

REVIEW: THE STEPS

I recommend doing planning and execution of technology using a process like the one I described in the last chapter. Here it is again, as a review. I covered the first two steps there and will cover steps 3 through 6 in this chapter.

1. **Roadmap your desired business outcomes** and how you will measure and monitor those outcomes.
2. **Analyze and choose technology products** required to achieve those outcomes.
3. **Decide on using in-house or external partners.**
4. **Sell the project internally,** beginning the hiring or partner evaluation after getting the internal go-ahead.
5. **Develop a project plan,** backing out of the date that will not move, highlighting dependencies, and specifying what milestones are and when they will be achieved.
6. **Implement the technology,** designing, building, and deploying it effectively.
7. **Monitor the result** and adjust regularly, as needed.

Before we go into the specifics of steps 3 through 6, however, I'll take a moment to discuss Counsel, one of the four capabilities critical to getting any given technology project over the line.

Have at Least One Trusted Advisor

In the TV shows *Game of Thrones* and *House of the Dragon*, characters act as "the hand of the king," the person who sits next to the king and helps him with difficult decisions. Kings aren't experts on specific topics; they become kings because they're in the right bloodline. So they appoint someone smart to sit next to them to help advise them on important decisions. The "hand of the king" has information and expertise that the king does not.

As I've said previously in the book, no single person can keep up with the pace of change in technology—not while also managing a technology team for a sports organization. So, to ensure you make the right decisions, I strongly recommend having at least one "hand of the king." This person can be internal or external; there can even be several individuals, depending on the topic. The key is for the "hand" to be both knowledgeable and trustworthy, someone who has gone through this before. Having the perspective on why you should go one way or the other will give you confidence and keep you sane.

Going through the advice process and writing up the evaluation of choices also gives you ammunition for later. If someone has a question, you can produce the document and explain why you made the choice that you did, whether that choice was in terms of money, flexibility, or anything else. The decision later becomes defensible in a way that quick, gut-level decisions do not.

The question then becomes, Should your advisor be internal or external?

Step 3: Decide on In-House or External Partners

Once you have chosen your technology, it's time to plan how it will be implemented. The first and most important strategic decision in implementation is whether to hire an outside partner or partners.

Some sports organizations will decide to build out an elite-level engineering organization. They will design and build most of what they need. These organizations have engineering, design, and product teams on payroll for digital technologies, and the array of skills needed keeps broadening over time. The investment is worthwhile to this organization, as they value internal capabilities and control.

Some organizations will go the opposite direction from necessity or preference, hiring external partners for nearly all technology needs. This strategy is nearly always best for a smaller or newer sports organization without the interest in building internal capabilities. Being able to dial up or dial down technology expenditures gives this organization more flexibility and more ability to make one big CapEx purchase last over time without much additional spending.

Of course, many organizations will sit somewhere in between, with a lean, professional team in house and external partners supplementing them as needed. (NASCAR refers to this approach as "NASCAR-izing technology," but I have seen many organizations of all sizes prefer this approach.) In fact, even the largest and most established organizations will go to an outside partner for expertise that they do not have in house. As Doug Perlman, a former lawyer who headed up media at the NHL and IMG before becoming the founder and CEO of Sports Media Advisors, says, "There are new areas of technology that require specialists. It's like a company that has a general counsel for day-to-day legal work but calls in outside counsel to work on significant or highly complex transactions. A company may have an IT department, but in all likelihood it will need to call in specialists when looking to upgrade their technology in everything from OTT, to security, to eCommerce, etc. Finding the right company means assessing their strengths, reviewing subject matter expertise, and insisting on evidence that they have successfully delivered projects that are similar to the one you are about to embark on." This is another area where the "hand of the king" can be very valuable.

Take stock of your internal capabilities and preferences and compare those with your planned efforts. Do you have the ability to do the work internally? Does your team have the time to do it in addition to their regular work operating the business? If the answer is no to either question, you will likely need to outsource. The technology has to work—that's table stakes—and has to run your business and support platforms that allow for advertising and partnership to pay the bills. Ensuring that it can be implemented correctly is nonnegotiable.

How Other Leaders Do It

Here are three sports technology leaders on how they decide to outsource technology work or to keep it in house:

> **Chris Marinak, chief operations & strategy officer, MLB:** "One of the benefits of us having control of our technology is that we're not beholden to the market. We always have an option of delivering these things ourselves. If something else emerges in the market that works really well and is great win-win for everybody, then sure, we can always lean more towards partners. But if that doesn't emerge, then we have a great stack in-house that we can use and tell the same story to our fans and create a great consumer experience that way as well."

> **Scott Gutterman, SVP digital & broadcast technologies, PGA TOUR:** "One of the things we've always felt . . . is

> we know golf really, really well, and we know golf technology really, really well. But especially back in 2012, that doesn't mean that we understood the cloud, right? It doesn't mean that we understood how to deploy code in the types of environments that we were getting ready to go into because we had never been in a cloud environment. So we had to . . . recognize that we needed expertise from outside the TOUR to come in and give us guidance and help us create the pathway forward."
>
> **Katee LaPoff, chief technology officer at Oak View Group:** "We manage vendors and we hire experts because we can't be experts in everything. Particularly when you think about geography and different data and protection privacy law and just the volume of events that we deal with, we would just have so many employees. So, we do definitely hire outsourced firms to help us be better at managing those individual things."

All of these leaders have significant capabilities and technology groups in house, but leaders often recognize their limits and outsource to supplement those limits. What limits does your team have? Which technologies would be better managed by outside groups with experience in that specific technology? Consider your budget, timelines, and other constraints as you make this decision.

Hire Carefully

All organizations—not just sports organizations—engage outside companies to do things that they don't know how to do or don't have the bandwidth to do. Sometimes the engagement goes well, but often the outsourced work comes in late and over budget, and may not even provide the desired outcome. If you wouldn't hire someone to build your house who has never built a house, don't hire a company to do a high-stakes sports technology project who has never done it before. Instead, look for someone with experience in the sports industry who has a track record of successful projects in your exact area. Ask for evidence of prior successful work for sports organizations you recognize. The established companies with the right experience will be happy to provide it.

Avoid RFPs

It is common practice for many companies to write a request for proposal (RFP) and send it out to companies who they believe have the capabilities to deliver. If there is one thing you take away from this book, I want it to be this: RFPs are a HORRIBLE way to pick an outside company to deliver complex technology projects.

There are three reasons for this truth:

1. To issue an RFP you need to provide the details a technology company needs to properly scope the project. But when you prescribe a detailed solution before going through a collaborative exercise to assess outcomes, you create blind spots. Do you really want them to deliver what you *think* you need, or what you actually need? You are asking experts to be experts, right? RFPs provide perverse incentives to those responding. Instead of helping you think through what you need, they focus on ways they can keep pricing as low as possible,

sometimes in unrealistic ways, because they know that is what you'll look at first. Less reputable companies may even reduce the price to unrealistic levels knowing that they'll charge you later with change requests for the things you did not consider.

2. RFPs are usually sent to companies that don't deliver technology solutions the same way. A product company will seek to fit what you've asked for into what their product does, a services company will use some combination of custom and existing technology, and a digital agency may plan to do the design but partner with others for required tech. The prices you get back have little value because they can't be compared apples to apples. Comparing the possible *outcomes* of working with these providers is impossible with the RFP process.
3. It's expensive. It's expensive to write RFPs (whether you do it internally or through a consultant) and expensive to respond to them. The work that goes into a quality RFP response can cost a respondent fifty thousand dollars (or more) in time and resources, and that does not consider opportunity cost. Most execs who send out RFPs have a pretty good instinct of who they are going to choose before they even receive a response. The other companies are referred to as "RFP fodder."

What if, instead, you took some important portion of the time/money you were going to put into an RFP and did one of two alternate approaches?

1. Split it between two or three of the companies you planned to review for the project. Give them a mini-project or problem to solve and two weeks to do it. This will give you a sense of the way each company works, how their culture "feels" to you, and the tools they use to deliver what they do. The process will also allow you to meet and work with key team members. At the end of the two weeks, you'll have a sense of whom you want to spend the next six to twelve months with on the actual project.
2. Or take the simpler, fast way: Go with the one with the best references. The experience others have had working with the companies you are considering is the most telling metric.

Ensure a Good Governance Structure

Just like the individuals working for you need to understand their roles, responsibilities, and the metrics they'll be judged against, so should any company working for you. Be clear about expectations and arrange for regular check-ins and reporting so that you can address issues early.

Step 4: Sell the Project Internally

In almost every organization, before you can move forward with a plan for a project that you want, you will have to advocate on behalf of *why* the organization should spend the resources to deliver the outcome you suggest. To do so successfully, you'll need to develop a clear scope for what you intend to do, the result it's going to create, and an estimation of the resources (time, people, money) required. Then, you will need to make your case and promote that case to the right people internally until they agree with you. (If they ultimately say no, you'll start back at the beginning and find a new path to your preferred business outcomes that you think will be signed off on.)

If the project or technology requires an outside provider, to make your case you'll need to know about how big of a check you'll need to write to that provider and have some idea of the timeline involved. If you're using internal resources, you'll need to know roughly how much it will cost in terms of effort, time, and actual money. All of these numbers will require a solid estimation process.

Estimation

If you are working with external companies and take my advice to avoid RFPs, you can still ask for estimates. They can provide those estimates based on high-level scope and the team of resources that will be required to deliver the project. These will usually come back as estimate ranges (i.e., plus or minus 30 percent) because the details matter, but they will at least give you a sense of project budget. If you plan to have the provider support the technology post-launch, you can ask for both CapEx (capital expense—build/delivery) and OpEx (operating expenses).

For internal projects, spend some time with your technical managers, considering who will do the work and how long it may take. Account for competing projects, internal initiatives, and "business as usual" work, as well as learning, development, holiday, and PTO requirements on your people, and make plans only with the remaining hours. Add your deadlines and milestones and compare the two to see if your plans are realistic. Since most humans are inherently bad at estimating accurately, and the problem is more pronounced the first few times that they work on a given task, build in buffer. For the first few projects, build in far more buffer, until estimations get more accurate. If you're not a technical person, you'll do this process with someone more senior, experienced, and technical to ensure that your sense of normal timelines is reasonable.*

Make absolutely sure that you consult with the people responsible for delivering the work in the end because it will build buy-in. Have them flag any dependencies that will affect the work that you may not have spotted. And keep in mind that the more complex the project is, the more difficult it will be to get an accurate estimate—so the more important meaningful buffer additions become.

Once you know the people assigned to each piece of the project and the length of time, you can determine the labor cost of your effort and compare that to other hard costs and their impact on your budget. To be clear, accurately estimating large-scale technology projects is a complicated process and is ideally done by leaders who have delivered similar projects before. Because the sports industry focuses on critical immovable dates, the degree of risk is high. Solid estimation must be followed by rigorous monitoring and project management.

---

* A popular alternative to this estimation process is to have the technical people doing the work make estimations about their time to deliver granular features. We usually refer to this as "bottom-up" estimating. I don't believe in this type of feature-level estimation because I've never seen it work. It also tends to take so much longer to build the estimation that the projects become less commercially viable.

Double Check Your Provider's Estimates

I strongly recommend that you look for evidence that the provider you are working with has done this type of work in your industry before. That will help to ensure their estimate is more accurate; if they're basing it on work they've done before in another industry, their estimate is likely less accurate.

When estimates are off, someone pays for the additional work. Either the provider will come back and ask for extra money, or they will eat the additional cost. Them eating the cost is actually not good for you, the client. When a provider has massively misestimated a project and now has little or no margin on it, they may not be able to afford to execute it correctly. The misestimation has put both of you in peril.

A friend of mine just built a huge home. Before he built it, he put the project out to bid, got an estimate, and selected a builder. Unfortunately, the company misestimated the project, and then COVID happened and the price of materials tripled, compounding the problem. My friend took the construction company to court to hold them to the original cost estimate. He won, but holding the builder to the original estimate wasn't a wise decision. Faced with massive losses, what motivation did the builder have to deliver a high-quality product? Did the builder even have the operating capital to do the work the right way? A few years later, my friend is still finding constant, systematic evidence of shoddy work done on the house. He's had multiple plumbing issues and a roof that wasn't done properly. The cost of the extra time, stress, and money he's putting into a subpar house is probably more than he saved in the end. Ultimately, no one won.

When you hire external providers to deliver enterprise-level technology, you are in it together. Think of it as a partnership: How you work together to adjust when conditions change (and they will) will determine whether you succeed. This just highlights the importance of picking the right providers—Ensure your provider has done this kind of work before and double-check references.

Step 5: Create and Update a Project Plan

Give me six hours to chop down a tree and I will spend the first four sharpening the axe.

—Abraham Lincoln

We have worked with organizations who previously hired external consulting companies to give recommendations and create project plans, but their plans often don't hold water in our industry. Many of these companies don't actually build technology, much less under the pressures of sports—but my organization does. We have learned that to deliver on time and on budget profitably in our industry, a granular project plan isn't optional.

Over the years, we've hammered out a consistent process to effectively deliver against dates that are not going to move, under the demands and constraints of the sports industry. We also don't have a product to sell; our priority is not getting clients to choose product A over B but rather helping define and deliver against specific outcomes. Since we've done that for the largest sports organizations in the world on immobile timelines, we've earned trust. Our recommendations carry weight. In the next pages, I'll summarize *how* we execute projects at this high level so that you can do the same.

The Competencies Model—Project Version

What is true at the roadmap level is also true at the project level: To succeed, you will need to ensure that you have all four competencies required to be successful. These can be taken up by experienced providers or by people within your organization, but all four must be present.

1. **Counsel.** Are you receiving the right counsel from the right people so that you fully understand the project and outcomes required?
2. **Choice.** In any project you'll have to make choices about how to proceed. Many of them will be technology based or hiring based, and you'll need a framework, expertise, counsel, or all three to choose well.
3. **Governance.** Do the people or provider(s) you've chosen have a clear idea of expectations? Do they understand how the outcomes you want align with the responsibilities they have and the metrics they'll be judged against? Do they know more granularly who is doing what and when? Who is in charge of the overall process, and which pieces?
4. **Execution.** In some ways, this is the most important part, but also the simplest if you've created a good project plan. Once you have talented project/product managers, designers, developers, and others, and they

have clear expectations, you can let the process, work ethic, and talent take over.

Confirm that your company has all four competencies and then begin your project plan.

What a Project Plan Should Include

The project plan should give a detailed view of how you're going to deliver your technology, by the date you need it and within the budget you've allotted (usually measured in resource utilization). You need not only a high-level plan for which projects will happen and when (what I earlier called the roadmap) but also a very detailed project plan for each individual project.

Each project plan should be detailed enough that each of its phases and iterations can be mapped to a visualized project chart (like a Gantt chart). You should be able to use your plan for a comprehensive view of the project, including all the following:

- hard delivery dates/deadlines
- requirements, features, and other deliverables sequenced to milestones
- dependency planning
- the people and resources allocated with clear responsibilities
- client or executive reviews
- time for quality assurance and user-acceptance testing processes
- buffer time, for the unexpected

Begin with the End

All project plans in our industry should be grounded in the critical delivery dates that almost always exist. These are the immobile realities that drive all other decision-making. So I recommend starting all planning with your end dates and working backward from there.

So, for example, when NBC Sports and NFL.com streamed the Super Bowl for the first time in 2012, more than 2 million people tuned in.* While that number was dwarfed by the 111 million total viewers that year, no broadcaster had supported that many concurrent views before in the history of sports. It was ambitious, and the innovative technology needed to be tested well in advance of kickoff time. At the time, this kind of endeavor required months of planning and was largely without the advantages of the advanced load testing we have today. Even with the most advanced technologies and protocols, there are many ways large events like this can run into issues. In November 2024, Netflix, the largest streaming platform in the world with around 275 million subscribers as of Q4 2024,† streamed the Jake Paul vs. Mike Tyson fight. The fight drew 65 million concurrent viewers, with 38 million concurrent streams in the US. And guess what? There were very visible technical issues as millions of fans experienced latency and buffering in their feed of the fight. Whether these issues could have been avoided with better planning is unclear. What is certain, however, is that a lack

* FOX Sports. 2012. "2.1 Million Viewers Live Stream Super Bowl Online." *FOX Sports*, February 8, 2012. https://www.foxsports.com/stories/nfl/2-1-million-viewers-live-stream-super-bowl-online.

† Nickinson, Phil. 2024. "The 10 Most Popular Streaming Services, Ranked by Subscriber Count." *Digital Trends*. October 2, 2024. https://www.digitaltrends.com/home-theater/most-popular-streaming-services-by-subscribers/.

of technology planning around large-scale sporting events can be disastrous.

Again, there will be unexpected circumstances. How you plan for risk mitigation and recovery means significantly less painful issues.

Step 6: Implement the Technology

Successful implementation requires rigor, with clear processes and governance. Everyone knows who is responsible for what, and when, and delivers accordingly.

This is a book about the business of sports technology, not the specifics of how to build technology, so I will assume you can execute with good planning.

Step 7: Measure, Monitor, and Adjust

The last critical part of any technology project is to measure your progress against your outcomes regularly and adjust your approach as necessary until you reach the desired state and set of results. Besides the need for preventative systems reliability engineering (SRE) practices (which I will cover in the next chapter), avoiding a "set it and forget it" mindset is probably the biggest hurdle for most organizations. Many executives cannot fathom that they'll spend (sometimes) millions of dollars on technology and yet still have to continue to adjust and maintain it for them to realize the full value of the investment.

Once a large capital project is deployed, the effort is just beginning—you are simply shifting from the CapEx phase to the OpEx phase. The sooner you accept the long-term nature of the relationship you'll have with your technology, the better.

Measuring KPIs and Monitoring Resources

Whatever KPIs you are attaching to the definition of success for the project, those KPIs should be measured and reviewed consistently. If a project fails to progress as expected, the team needs to adjust. For example, if a platform fails to adequately serve content in a way that will deliver the expected level of increased ticket sales, consider how you should either adjust the technology itself or the user's journey through it.

There may be nothing more important in a large-scale technology project than monitoring and managing resource progress and allocation. Next League focuses heavily on the systems and processes that allow for the granular monitoring and management of team resources. Project and resource management software, when used correctly, can automatically track your teams' work progress against the plan. If a given developer is moving through work slower than planned, or spending more or fewer hours than expected, that dynamic can be flagged and identified early. If it is likely to cause an issue for the project as a whole, we can make adjustments in time. Not all providers monitor at this level, but it can be the difference between failure and profitability. With the right project and resource management software and processes, leaders can monitor progress and utilization so that when they notice an issue, there can be a response before a cascade of consequences snowballs, putting a project's due date in peril.

If you don't monitor your project at this level, it's possible that you'll make it to the finish line on time, but lacking this process rigor introduces significant risk in the sports industry. If a developer is blocked for weeks, or pulled off the project by someone who didn't report it, all the dependencies connected to that developer may begin to unravel. Without the proper level of visibility, dozens of project staff members and multiple teams of providers may be going in the wrong direction or, worse, unable to move forward at all. You can easily lose millions of dollars in resourcing before noticing a problem. This cannot happen—so you monitor.

Reporting

I recommend reviewing the overall project status at least weekly. In our organization, we have project managers report weekly on the project health relative to the following key areas:

- **Expectation status.** How is the experience of the client or business owner? Are they getting the result they "signed up for"? These are important questions whether you are an external provider or an internal team managing executive stakeholders.
- **Project status.** What percentage complete are the project timeline and scope? In other words, will this ship arrive in the desired location on time?
- **Resource utilization.** Do we have the right team members and size of team? Do we need to scale up or down?
- **Budget.** How are we trending relative to the allocated budget? If we are off, why are we off?
- **Team health.** How's our team feeling? Overworked teams are common in the sports technology business—but this is often when processes are skipped and mistakes happen.

There are also forward-looking dynamics to monitor:

- What risks and issues do we anticipate? How can we mitigate them?
- Which milestones are coming up that we need to get in front of? (Launch, post-launch, live event, etc.)

Once projects complete implementation and launch, we prioritize retrospectives with our internal team and clients so we can reflect, get feedback, and implement changes for next time.

If you are managing the project, I recommend creating a checklist to review the project in those key areas directly every week. Knowing about an issue early gives you or your project manager insight into ramping team members up or down. It also gives your organization time to spot problems and mitigate them and you time to make strategic choices.

Adjusting the Plan in Real Time

Circumstances will change over time, and so should your project plan. Since you are monitoring that plan closely and reviewing its status every week, you will notice when the project health slips. When something happens, you'll address the problem immediately. That's how you deliver against budgets and timeframes that don't move.

However, even with normal amounts of buffer built into the system, everybody will inevitably reach a situation where the math doesn't math. With the burn rate you have and the adjustments you have made, you know you won't complete the work in the time you have. Or a truly unforeseeable situation arises, like it did for Next League when a war broke out in Ukraine, where we had developers. We helped them in the ways we could, and we helped some of them get out and settle in other countries, but without the fortitude of the team members affected and the planning we already had in place, it could have been very disruptive. Fortunately, this example did not lead to any significant project issues, but we did have to manage an unexpected event, and unexpected events will happen.

Descope as Needed

There are three levers in any project management approach: time, scope, and cost. If time and cost cannot change, as they usually cannot in our industry, we are left with only one option to change: scope. When situations come up that affect the project, the only option to still deliver fully functional technology on deadline is to descope (i.e., remove functionality from the technology roadmap). This is why it is so critical to plan based on priorities and for each iteration to have "nice to have" features that can be cut or delayed if necessary.

If you plan well and deliver the critical features and functionality on time, the rest can often wait until the next release. Begin with foundational technology and functionality and then shift to features you are contractually obligated to deliver based on partnerships, for example. Everything else should be on the descoping table when and if that need arises.

So, for example, if you have committed to delivering a mobile application to stream the Olympics, the technology has to work when the Olympics begin. That's nonnegotiable. But, depending on the requirements of the project, descoping features like a Large Language Model (LLM)-powered chat assistant or detailed data visualizations could be options.

Descoping is how you consistently deliver excellent work under the demands of our industry and preserve strong relationships with fans.

The Degree of Rigor in Testing Is a Strategic Decision

The two last steps in the software development life cycle are quality assurance testing and user acceptance testing. These are steps that can be streamlined, if you choose to do so and are willing to accept the cost in terms of risk to the quality of your product.

I have been in more than one situation where the teams involved decided to spend less time testing so that we could deliver more features by the launch date. The key here is that we were prepared for the consequences. We expected we would have more issues with deployment and more problems on the day of the event, and we ramped up SRE measures to compensate. (See the next chapter.)

Keep in mind that the more innovative the technology, the more likely it is to break when a critical mass of fans descend on it, and the more critical testing is. For truly innovative technology, plan accordingly.

Planning Decreases Risk

If you don't have a plan for how you're going to get from point A to point B, considering all the dynamics that you face, I cannot guarantee you'll fail. There's always a small chance it will work—even a blind squirrel finds a nut now and then. But if you have a solid plan that you implement with rigor, you significantly increase the odds that you are going to succeed.

The parameters of our industry are unforgiving. You have to deliver technologies that work, under some of the most demanding loads in the world, with limited resources. You can't throw an unlimited number of people against a problem with a budget attached. You can't purchase different technology when the CapEx budget is spent. The decisions you make on what to choose and how to implement, then, are critically important.

Ensure you have counsel, technology choice rigor, good governance, and solid execution practices for each project. Establish a robust project plan, rigorous implementation, and constant monitoring and adjustment. If you hire an outside consultant, they should be able to provide you with updates and artifacts that prove the project is where it needs to be. If you put a project manager in charge of a technology deployment inside your organization, the same is true there as well. It's not enough to say the right thing; there needs to be proof of monitoring.

If you want a predictable result, you must have both the implementation plan and the expectations management plan—and partner with others who do the same—to get there.

Of course, it's not enough to deploy technology correctly; there must also be a plan in place for what to do when there's an inevitable technical problem in the middle of a live event. In the next chapter, I'll walk you through how to manage technology risk using systems reliability engineering (SRE) practices.

CHAPTER FOUR: ACTION LIST

In this chapter, I described how to put all the pieces together to create rigorous planning. Now, do the legwork to create the following:

- **Counsel.** Deciding on who you'll work with and having the proper counsel to execute a project is critical.

- **Choice.** Understand internal dynamics; you'll need to get internal buy-in for both what you want to do and how you'll do it. Do yourself a favor and document your plan, who approved it, and when.
- **Governance.** Have a plan for both the project you envision in its initial state and your proposed path to get there, including who is responsible for what. Remember that big technology projects are massive expectations-management exercises—so overcommunicate, early and often.
- **Execution.** Executing against dates that don't move is difficult, but a successful launch does not mean you are done. Have a plan to measure and monitor the results you expected at the beginning of the process. Then, go through a formal learning and improvement process to capture what you can do better next time.

5

TECH DOESN'T JUST WORK

It was the first morning of the first day of one of the largest sporting events in the US. My team had worked hard, with sleepless nights, and the technology we had built for the event was ready. We had designed an authentication gate for event highlights so the sports property could gather data on their fans. Simply providing a name and email would allow hundreds of thousands of users access to highlights in real time. The gate was working well, and we were collecting email addresses for the database smoothly. Everything was going exactly as we'd planned.

Then, suddenly, no one could get to the highlights. As is often the case when technology stops working, there was no obvious cause.

It was seven thirty in the morning. Every few seconds that elapsed, thousands of users were unable to access the content. The clock was ticking, and executive leadership at the sports property was not happy. Since a partner was funding the area of the platform that delivered the highlights, if that area couldn't be accessed, revenue could be at risk. After a few minutes, we figured out the problem was with the gating technology, so we turned that part of the system off while we were troubleshooting. To the outside world, a relatively small number of people had a brief issue before the highlights came back on. For our team and the client, there was stress and confusion.

We spent hours troubleshooting in the wrong functionality because the real issue had been ruled out much earlier. The gate we were using relied on an authentication API to function. (APIs serve as structured interfaces that enable secure, rate-limited communication between applications, often with authentication layers.)

Unlike businesses where technical requirements are spread evenly across full days, large sporting events focus on three-to-four-hour live windows when events take place and most of their revenue is generated. During the live window of the event, API calls can go from almost none to hundreds of thousands of calls per second. Many commercial systems aren't built to manage that kind of load—in fact, companies responsible for resource management may eventually decline access outright to help manage cost and limit risk. (The kinds of rapid spikes in traffic common in the sports industry look just like a denial-of-service attack from bad actors designed to break systems.) Because of this reality, part of the preparation that takes place in system reliability engineering (SRE) is in anticipating where systems will be taxed by increased load.

During the systems design process months before, our systems architect had inquired of the company running authentication if there were API call limits. There were not. Unfortunately, in the weeks since, that policy had changed. A previously unknown limit on API calls effectively shut down a key component of our technology. In relatively short order, we identified and resolved the issue but not without a good deal of scrambling by engineering and frustration from senior client stakeholders.

Policy and/or protocol changes made by third-party platforms are often not communicated well to the communities of developers who leverage them. It's not reasonable to expect software engineers to scour randomly updated technical documentation, especially when they are already familiar with how the technology functions and are operating against a critical date that cannot move. But the impact of policy changes can be significant.

I recently told this story to a roomful of technology officers at large sports organizations, and many in the room smiled. "It's always something," a CTO with twenty years of experience said, raising his beer in solidarity. Two other senior tech leaders chimed in with their own stories of how, even with the appropriate amount of planning and rigor in the process, there are just too many moving parts to account for every eventuality.

INTERLOCKING PIECES

The crisis you have to worry about most is the one you don't see coming.

—Mike Mansfield, senate majority leader from 1961–1977

Deploying new technology is like solving a puzzle. We design systems from puzzle pieces and integrate them with other pieces. As I've said, this type of development massively expands what can be built within the time and budget constraints that are present in all sports organizations. The downside is that this introduces more and more external dependencies, which carry with them new risks.

Most experienced technology leaders in sports organizations don't sit around and hope nothing goes wrong; they actively plan for risk mitigation and recovery. They institute a continuous cycle of learning from the issues that inevitably arise, and they create rigorous processes to ensure stability.

Scott Gutterman of the PGA TOUR talks about this process of planning for and adapting to the inevitable challenges of technology. In 2012, OMNIGON was a part of the team responsible for standing up all new PGA TOUR–owned digital technology infrastructure, and we were all getting ready to press the proverbial button for it to go live. The button was pushed . . . and nothing happened. The whole team spent two-and-a-half hours at two o'clock in the morning trying to figure out why the new PGATOUR.com wasn't showing up. As Gutterman put it, "It turned out that in a DNS file somewhere, somebody had forgotten a semicolon . . . And it's funny because from that point on, you have to learn patience. You have to learn that things are going to happen."

Gutterman continued: "I always tell my teams and new people, we're going to have problems. There's always going to be an issue . . . But what I really try to do is not have the same problem three times . . . You might have the same problem as much as twice, but if you have it three times, you're not learning. You're not paying attention to what you need to be adjusting to, or reflecting on what you need to do." Gutterman says he works hard to make sure that his internal people *and* his providers are given extra bandwidth to be able to manage unexpected issues as they come up. "Because in the end, you're putting together a big puzzle, which largely shouldn't look like a puzzle to anybody [on the outside, but rather simply] displaying scores or leaderboards or video [in a way that feels coherent and unified]."

Gutterman recommends planning for the complexity of technology right from the very beginning so that you "don't paint yourself in a corner. Build on/off switches for everything that you can . . . so if a particular scoring feed goes down, it doesn't take down your entire experience." Gutterman says that in the case of the PGA TOUR, for example, if TOURCast isn't working, he turns it off until his people can fix it without affecting their website or apps. He also gives the team time to think about how to make technology modular and to create the systems that don't cascade when there's an issue. The planning takes extra time, but the benefits are immense.

According to Gutterman, "Not everything on the internet actually works. Like, you flip a switch and off it goes. That first night taught us that lesson. But I think it's constantly one that we are being reminded of, whether that's through our own efforts or missteps . . . I think you can get complacent." After one of his executives made the comment that mishaps don't happen at big companies, Gutterman rattled off a list of all the outages that happen week in and week out, from big social media companies to big cloud companies. In just the last year, it was a long list.

Just like in the example of the PGA TOUR, Next League plans for inevitable issues and responds quickly. We spend a tremendous amount of time on risk mitigation and recovery planning within our systems reliability engineering practice (SRE). You should do the same.

Technology isn't something smart organizations build and launch and then walk away from. It's a living thing that requires feeding and watering. To stay functional and to continue to provide good experiences for the fans, it will need to be properly and consistently maintained.

THE ADVANTAGES OF SYSTEMS RELIABILITY ENGINEERING (SRE)

The biggest companies in the world spend major time and money ensuring their technology is available to those who rely on it and that problems are resolved immediately. That's why Google established their Systems Reliability Engineering (SRE) practice in 2003 and published a book on their methods in 2013.* In Google's own words, the practice keeps "important, revenue-critical systems up and running despite hurricanes, bandwidth outages, and configuration errors."†

Next League's SRE team describes their work in the following way: "We believe in thoroughness, preparation, and documentation . . . We cultivate an awareness of what could go wrong and nurture a strong desire to prevent it," as well as respond in real time to troubleshoot issues as they do arise, for whatever reason.

SRE, which includes practices such as SLA (Service Level Agreement), SLO (Service Level Objective), and SLI (Service Level Indicator),

---

* Ely, Ryan. 2022. "The Origins of SRE from the Director of SRE Education at Google." DevOps Institute. October 4, 2022. https://www.devopsinstitute.com/blog-the-origins-of-sre-from-the-director-of-sre-education-at-google/#:~:text=I%20think%20it's%20first%20important,start%20at%20Google%20in%202003.

† "The History of SRE." n.d. https://sre.google/.

error budgets, chaos testing, and rollback mechanisms to ensure uptime, is standard in any industry where technology *must* work, and that should include sports technology. The same practices that protect the technology that produces revenue for Google and nearly every other large technology company in the world should also protect yours. The stakes of failure are too high: A small outage that's immediately dealt with may have no consequences, but if video streaming goes down for the Super Bowl, you can lose millions in revenue every minute.

A few key issues drive the need for SRE mitigation:

- legacy systems
- human error
- third-party updates
- bad actors
- the reality of modern software needing constant change to stay relevant

I'll start with the last issue, which is by far the greatest.

THE MYTH OF THE PERFECT CODE

Most modern software is constantly changing. Whether it's web based, app based, and/or connected to the cloud, most software depends on other software and systems and connections to that software and systems. The constant changing is deliberate—it makes all our software more secure and less prone to hacking or data breaches. But the constant software, API, and dependency changes around us mean that sports technology cannot remain static either.

In other words, the most perfect software in the world will become outdated over time as the world changes around it. Sometimes there are actually bugs caused by issues with the way code was written, but more often, it's the influence of hundreds or thousands of external dynamics outside your span of control that will ultimately impact your technology.

Third-Party APIs Change Without Notice

Those technologies that depend on third-party services may be more secure or have additional features that stand up to the massive demands of sporting events, but their underlying reality may change without notice. Years ago, Facebook (Meta), for example, was known for making API changes without informing those who rely on them. These types of changes can and do interrupt the expected flow or format that a development team has planned for and introduce breakage. Having a team that can promptly handle a breakage matters, especially in the live window.

HUMAN ERROR

No matter how competent your people are, they will occasionally make mistakes. The team responsible for the PGA TOUR platform forgot a semicolon on a DNS file, and it broke their deployment until they solved the problem. I've had sports executives from other organizations tell me stories of other problems caused by human error. It happens to us all.

A few years ago, my team was adding features to a mobile app for a very large sports organization, an app that had already had millions of downloads. One of our developers was testing a feature and believed incorrectly that he was working within the development environment of the application rather than the production (live) one. (There are processes that ensure this doesn't happen 99.9 percent of the time, but he didn't follow them.) It wasn't malicious, but that didn't matter. He sent a push notification that said "push one for [his name]" to the home screens of millions of people's phones.

While I laugh when I tell the story now, at the time it wasn't funny—we almost lost a major client over it. We've never made that mistake before or since, but errors have real consequences in terms of money and reputation.

I can talk all day long about the processes and protocol to catch errors in my organization, and others can tell you about theirs too. Errors are almost always caught long before they go into production—but human error can never entirely be removed from the equation. Every company on earth is made up of people, and people make mistakes.

No Way to Eliminate Human Error

For those who say that artificial intelligence (AI) writing code will eliminate human error, I say, not so fast. Humans train models and write the prompts that AI leverages to do what it does. When we get to artificial general intelligence (AGI), code will be cleaner and faster, but the potential for human error will not go away . . . unless humans do (and let's hope we do not).

Humans and machines both cause errors, and rather than ignore the reality, it's better to plan for the errors in advance. SRE exists not only to keep software up-to-date but also to control risk and minimize damage from any rare errors that somehow manage to go into production. It's much better to have a system in place to deal with the errors promptly than to ignore the possibility of occasional human error.

LEGACY SYSTEMS HOLD MORE RISK

Legacy systems often cause more breakages because of the substantial technical debt they may carry in their codebase. They are often written in languages now out-of-date, and new programmers may struggle to understand and update those languages. The person or people who created the system likely have not properly documented it and may be long gone. Figuring out *any* changes in the system can, as a result, be highly inefficient and complex. Since the legacy system may be poorly understood, there can be unexpected downstream effects on other systems that take time to troubleshoot. All of this means that older legacy systems are, by their nature, costly to operate.

When compared to modern interfaces, the older technologies may also have sharp limitations and fail more often when an external API or program changes, since older software was often *not* intended to work in a world of constant change.

Even so, there can be substantial reasons to keep those systems running. As mentioned earlier, it can be expensive and risky to replace something that has been working for a long time. The system may hold decades of critical organizational information or support business-critical functions. There may not yet be the budget to modernize. Yet, the larger and more complex the system, and the more external dependencies there are, the more opportunity there is for failure.

NOTHING IS IMPENETRABLE

The sports industry is one of the most high profile in the world, and we will attract our share of problems and bad actors. Sometimes systems will be trampled by a thundering herd of well-meaning fans, with too many people at a time for the system to handle. Sometimes, a bad actor can target sports organizations intending to do harm. No system is impenetrable, and everything has weaknesses. In fact, the organizations that we as humans most trust with our personal information, like Equifax* and the Pentagon,† still get successfully hacked at times, despite extensive preventative work to the contrary.

Adding good SRE practices not only significantly decreases the risk of problems and bad actors successfully affecting your systems, but it also puts a plan in place to quickly respond when something happens. In a world where bad actors and high-traffic loads can pop up unexpectedly, SRE provides risk mitigation.

MAKING CAREFUL INVESTMENT DECISIONS

I would argue that nearly all technology in the sports industry should have measurable value: It should produce revenue, create great fan experiences, enable partnerships and advertisers, reduce risk in some way, etc. Otherwise, why invest at all?

I recommend spending extra time to truly think through *why* you're making technology decisions. For example, I often talk to sports organizations who want to launch a native mobile app. When I ask them why, there is often no reason other than simply to have

---

* Egan, John. 2022. "Five Years After the Equifax Data Breach, How Safe Is Your Data?" Bankrate. September 9, 2022. https://www.bankrate.com/credit-cards/news/how-safe-is-your-data/#protect.

† Roush, Ty. 2024. "Russian Hackers Breached 632,000 DOJ and Pentagon Email Addresses in Massive MOVEit Cyberattack, Report Says." *Forbes*, June 3, 2024. https://www.forbes.com/sites/tylerroush/2023/10/30/russian-hackers-breached-632000-doj-and-pentagon-email-addresses-in-massive-moveit-cyberattack-report-says/.

an app—they basically want to present their website to the fan in another format. I always challenge that decision-making. Building and then maintaining two code bases (iOS and Android) is not worth it when you have not established the business metrics that justify the investment. That's not to say that I don't support app development—it's a huge part of our business—but our team will push clients through the process of analyzing the ROI before supporting the investment. That ROI, in whatever form it takes, should be well thought through and well designed.

If it's important enough to produce millions in revenue, support fan experiences to build relationships, and enable partnerships and advertising, it's probably important enough to protect with an approach to SRE.

Good Documentation

As the organization grows and deals with problems, there should be more processes put in place to support formal learning. This ensures that, as Gutterman mentioned earlier, the same mistakes aren't made more than twice. Many organizations like to build playbooks on how to respond to different problems both in advance of a launch and during a launch process, as reference material to speed responses and prevent issues. These playbooks can also support prophylactic measures to prevent issues before a launch.

Documentation can be a large investment in terms of time, but it's often one of the most effective long-term risk mitigation tools. The more of the system and its quirks that you can write down, the less time your engineering team will need to spend triaging when a problem arises. Documentation also prevents the risk that your whole system becomes unfixable if a key technical staff member gets hit by a bus tomorrow.

Of course, you may not be able to document *everything*. In fact, it's not practical to even try. Focus on the most impactful risks in terms of revenue and impact and cover those first.

PRIORITIZING FANS AND PARTNERS

Ultimately, sports organizations are entirely and completely reliant on the most loyal consumers on the planet: the fans. The relationship with the fan drives the entire business. So acquiring, retaining, and growing your fan base, and providing that fan base with excellent experiences, is the center of what we do. Even partnerships are only there because of the fans.

If you're not willing to make the investments required to ensure the quality of the experiences fans have across your brand, then you might be in the wrong business. The proper design, development, and operation of the technology protects the business model of the sporting organization. It's not optional.

WHAT'S NEXT

Now that I've talked about how to think about, plan for, implement, and protect your technology purchases, it's time to move to the specifics of technology. In the next chapter, I'll walk you through the technologies that allow for partnerships and advertising, which create the revenue that can help pay for everything else.

CHAPTER FIVE: ACTION LIST

In this chapter, I described how to put all the pieces together to create rigorous planning. Now, do the legwork to create the following:

- **Counsel.** Consider who can help guide the size of the investment in time, process, and resources your organization will need to prevent and address breakages and what you can afford to spend prophylactically.
- **Choice.** Determine what level of support processes you will fund and when. Can you outsource SRE support for critical events, or should you spin up support in house?
- **Governance.** Have a plan for what to do when something inevitably breaks and who is responsible for what at that time. Make it clear whose roles include technology risk mitigation and how.
- **Execution.** Consider creating a playbook and documentation to support continuing practices and run drills. Then, as Gutterman said at the beginning of the chapter, check in regularly to ensure that no mistake happens three times. Learning must be part of the regular rhythm of technical work.

PART TWO

APPLYING TECHNOLOGY IN THE BUSINESS OF SPORTS

6

PARTNERSHIPS AND ADVERTISING

Between 2012 and 2013, OMNIGON built an interactive media platform for a high-profile sporting event.* The idea was to seed a bracket with memorable moments from a tournament as it happened and to allow the moments to be voted on by fans to determine the best moment from the tournament. Fans who tweeted with the correct hashtags, mentioning the tournament's presenting partner, could help their favorite moment advance in the rankings. The partnership paid for the technology and produced a nice margin for the sporting event.

Hundreds of thousands of people directly interacted with the competition on the organization's website leaderboard, with millions seeing the conversation on Twitter with the partner's name. From a brand standpoint, all that engagement was immensely valuable.

---

* As a reminder, this is the company I cofounded, and that's now a part of Next League.

Twitter was popular at the time but still new enough that standards and protocols were not fully mature. No one involved in the contest—OMNIGON, the sports organization, or the partner's executives—anticipated the wave of interest and, more importantly, the wave of bad actors who sought to game the system. Bots were programmed to flood the contest with tweets, skewing the voting and generally creating chaos for all involved. The chaos became associated with the hashtags mentioning the partner, a major brand problem. We fixed the issue, but it went from a huge win for the partner to, ultimately, a big mea culpa for us.

Of course, that project wasn't the only one having problems. Around the same time, a major sports team ran a similar fan bracket allowing fans to vote for their favorite cheerleaders. The same thing happened there: One of the cheerleaders had a boyfriend in software development who worked out how to code a Twitter bot. Everyone else got a few thousand votes, and she got 1.2 million. The brand partner was not pleased with the obvious automation. But every fan bracket built beginning in the next year, including ours, planned for the problem and built in alerts and throttles.

While the rest of this chapter will cover partnership and advertising in sports, I will point out here that fan ecosystems are unpredictable. Any technology that interacts with large numbers of fans will need to consider not only what may go wrong from a technology point of view but also how the fans might interact with it nefariously—and make arrangements to limit that potential risk. Keeping the partner happy is essential to success in this arena.

High-Stakes Technology

A person who never made a mistake never tried anything new.

—Albert Einstein

The technology involved in partnerships and advertising isn't usually harder or more complicated than other types of technology, but the stakes are higher. The partner expects a certain result because they have made an investment and attached their biggest asset, their brand, to the program. You can't fail to deliver. The same is true, to a lesser degree, of technology that supports advertisers. A large portion of the revenue that supports the entire organization may come from the technology you build.

Unfortunately, the situation is made more complicated by the nature of what many partners seek: innovation. Most partners want to associate their brands with things that the media and consumers will find new and innovative or, in a word, cool. The challenge with innovation is that it is, by its nature, new. Something that hasn't been done before, or at least not done often, will tend to break or fail more. It's also harder to anticipate how fans may interact with the tech and if that interaction will come in waves.

When delivering innovative solutions for partners, be prepared for the possibility, if not the eventuality, that some version of the work doesn't go the way you expect. The damage associated with a partner- or advertiser-oriented digital product isn't worse than any other digital product breakage. It's just more directly connected to money. The higher profile your sports brand is, the more fans you have and the more money partner exposure is worth. The same goes for the fallout if some important part of the experience you are delivering doesn't work. The more it's worth on the upside, the more it costs on the downside.

The good news is you can prevent or limit damage using good quality assurance and SRE practices. You can anticipate what might not work, whether technologically or on the business side, and put plans in place to mitigate risk. When you design and build innovative technology that massive audiences will experience, planning is not optional.

When it comes to partnership and advertising, it has to work.

THE OPPORTUNITY

Most of the organizations Next League works with are net positive on their technology investments because of partnerships. You too should be able to create partnerships that pay for nearly all your fan experience technology. (The inward-facing technology powering your business may remain a cost center, but this is standard in almost all industries.) If you're not creating partnership strategies to pay for the technologies that power your fan experiences, you should.

Some of the biggest brands in the world want to partner with sporting organizations because of the loyalty and excitement of their fans. They hope that the perception of their brand will benefit from being associated with a fan's favorite teams or leagues. With any luck, the love that the fan has for the sport will transfer to them. They are eager to partner, and the money is there.

Some of the biggest technology companies in the world, Amazon, Apple, Google, and Microsoft, all have a market capitalization of over $2 trillion as of this writing. These technology companies are now some of the biggest partners to sports organizations and have even gotten into the media rights space. Apple just crossed a $3.5 trillion valuation, and they're in the sports business: They own all MLS games and Friday Night Baseball. Alphabet bought the NFL Sunday ticket package, the most expensive thing that the NFL sells, for YouTube for $2 billion per year.*

Technology companies are obvious partners of sports technology products and fan experiences, but their goals and needs are different from many traditional organizations. Traditional partnership salespeople may need additional help understanding the needs and priorities of technology companies. These companies will care less about traditional inventory such as logo placement and signage; instead, they want to partner with sports organizations who can help them demonstrate what differentiates their tech offering from their competitors. For example, Amazon wants to associate themselves with the NFL Next Gen Stats because the tech implementation clearly illustrates the power of their technology.

THE DIFFERENCE BETWEEN PARTNERSHIPS AND ADVERTISING

Partnerships are a quality game: relationships built one-on-one with companies based on their needs. They may include traditional ad placement and traditional inventory (like event signage or hospitality) as well as partnerable technology products. Creating an excellent experience for the partner is paramount, with expectations management being critical. The *quality* of the relationship matters

---

* Smith, Gerry; Love, Julia, *The Associated Press*. 2022. "Get Ready Watch Your NFL Games on YouTube After Yet Another Tech Company Steps Into the Football Arena." *Fortune*. December 22, 2022. https://fortune.com/2022/12/22/watch-nfl-youtube-alphabet-deal/.

greatly, and custom and innovative technology experiences can generate more and better partner relationships.

In contrast, advertising is a numbers game: It's about the combination of quality *and the quantity* of eyeballs you can acquire. The more specific the target audience is and the more of those specific people see a given ad, the more value there is. Advertisers can track who is viewing and clicking on their ads, and they can maximize conversion (clicks) using technology and psychology. Ads are still literally sold in thousands of views (CPM = *cost per mille*, or cost per thousand impressions), or per click, with more views and/or clicks meaning more value. Simply put, partnerships are quality one-to-one relationships; advertising is about numbers.

For large audiences, offering digital advertising can provide significant revenue. But it can also irritate the fans when done to excess. How easily your fans are irritated should and will affect how much advertising you decide to offer. Smaller, newer sports organizations and media sites may forgo the incremental revenue associated with advertising due to their lack of scale, focusing instead on a few key partnerships. Even some organizations with great scale, like The Masters Tournament and the USGA U.S. Open, eschew advertising in favor of high-value partnerships and the cleanest possible experience for fans. They have chosen partnerships only with companies like Mercedes-Benz, AT&T, and Rolex to protect the perception of their brand.

But for many sports properties, advertising serves an important purpose and, when done properly, can yield meaningful revenue for the business. Like everything else in your digital technology ecosystem, how you approach advertising should be based on your business goals and what your fans expect (and will tolerate).

THE BASICS OF ADVERTISING

Ad revenue has been an important part of the P&L for sports media platforms for decades, and it is a complicated topic both conceptually and technically. Because of this, I am going to touch on how the sports media advertising ecosystem operates, but only at a high level. It all starts with the fact that the digital media side of a sports organization can attract significant audiences and demographic profiles that are important to advertisers. In short, advertisers want to show up where sports fans are.

Sports organizations can sell advertising on their digital properties directly or as part of partnerships. The challenge for these organizations is that digital media platforms have spikes in traffic during their live events when all the action is taking place, and most advertisers want their messaging to be spread out over days or weeks. Advertisers will cap the number of ads to display on a single day or week, which means that those spikes in traffic can cause the platform to run out of ads.

CHANGES IN THE ADVERTISING INDUSTRY

Right now in advertising, the CPM model is in a race to the bottom. As more and more content is available on the internet, ads flood everyone's experiences, and the volume means CPMs go down. Because of the strong loyalty of your fan base, sporting organizations may be affected less by these changes than other properties, but they will be affected.

Does that mean advertising is going away? I don't believe that to be the case—for decades, many people in the media industry have been saying the advertising model will eventually stop working. Despite this, every year, advertising remains; it has adapted and changed steadily since the *Mad Men* days of the 1950s and '60s. Unless the behavior of human beings changes radically, I predict we'll still have advertising for decades to come. Shown an ad enough times, an important portion of an audience will click the ad, and some will buy the product. Advertising works.

In the movie *Jurassic Park,* the scientists say that cloning dinosaurs is safe because they are only making females, meaning they can't reproduce on their own. Upon hearing this, Jeff Goldblum's character responds ominously, "If there's one thing that the history of evolution has taught us is that life will not be contained. Life breaks free. It expands to new territories; it crashes through barriers." If we swap out the word *life* for *advertising*, the line still works. According to ad media giant GroupM, the global advertising spend will grow 7.8 percent in 2024 to $989.8 billion and increase a further 6.8 percent in 2025 to $1.1 trillion.* There are no signs that the advertising market is going away.

PARTNERSHIPS: A GUIDE TO SUCCESS

All sports organizations need partnerships to pay the bills. The opportunity right now in sports technology is to craft products to be partnerable from the beginning. The right partnerships will pay for technology implementations and cement relationships with fans, if sold and managed well.

Partnerships—and to some degree, relationships with larger advertisers—are an exercise in expectations management. The

---

* Szalai, Georg. 2024. "Global Ad Revenue to Surpass $1 Trillion in 2025 as GroupM Boosts 2024 Forecast for U.S., China." *The Hollywood Reporter*, June 10, 2024. https://www.hollywoodreporter.com/business/business-news/2024-global-advertising-forecast-groupm-trillion-2025-1235917863/.

experience of working with your team, both from a sales and a technology perspective, should be positive. The partner should know what to expect clearly, and that should be delivered on time. The partner should also have a feeling of confidence and trust that you *can* deliver from the very first moment they talk to you.

To protect your partnerships, ensure that your sales team's promises are accurate to what you can actually deliver. Many teams that are involved commercially in selling these partnerships are not familiar with the technology that will fulfill against the partnership, so they will sometimes overpromise on either functionality or commercial viability. So, to avoid misunderstandings and impossible contracts, include technologists and designers in any product ideation work from the beginning, before anything is signed.

A key part of expectations management isn't just delivering the value, however—it's making the partner *feel* that they received the value. **Understand what matters to them and deliver that.** Meet or exceed their expectations. Above all, communicate. Partners should be updated when experiences go live and should see those experiences being delivered well. Look for opportunities to deliver a perception of value whenever possible and communicate frequently. Ask questions and listen.

How Another Leader Does It

I recently had the opportunity to chat with Jeff Price, CEO of the Heisman Trophy Trust and formerly chief commercial officer of the PGA of America. Jeff's had a fascinating career that has spanned working on both the buying (brand) side of partnerships and the selling side. Jeff put it this way:

> I used to hate when I was on the buying side, the cookie cutter, everybody seeing the same pitch, not doing the research, whether it was at Gatorade or Mastercard. What are the drivers? What's the return you're looking for? How does it fit into the marketing mix? And so our team, we like to think of every partnership that we build as holistically being built based on the feedback that we get by asking the right questions of our partners. Understanding what their objectives are, are they aligned with our mission? If you're a Ryder Cup partner, do you believe in the totality of the event?. . . [It's important] being able to build partnerships that are done from the ground up, asking the right questions, understanding objectives, and then being a good partner.
>
> Seth Waugh, our former CEO, always said, we want to be the best partner for our partners. And the only way you can do that is if you ask questions, if you listen . . . I think about our great partner at Rolex and we've got a very long-term deal, but every year we sit and strategically plan what's important to [them] this year. What are the things that we need to be focused against? Companies evolve . . . If you think holistically, if you think with longevity, and you listen to each other, good things can happen.

Of course, partnerships are about more than just relationship building and expectations management (as critical as those aspects are). Here are some general principles about how partnerable opportunities generally work, and how to get the most out of them. (For a more complete treatment of my full philosophy of serving customers and securing revenue see my other book, *Zero Sales: Generating Services Revenue Without Selling.*)

Build Experiences

While the details of an offering matter, buyers commit based on how you make them *feel*, and emotions are best driven through storytelling. How can you spend the time to create unique experiences on behalf of the partner, and tell the story of those experiences, in a way that makes the partner want to buy?

By far the most common form of technology partnership will be for a digital product or fan experience that's built on behalf of a partner. These should be crafted with what matters to the partner in mind and should align with their business goals (see Creative Alignment below). Typically, these experiences are hosted on your owned-and-operated technology platforms, things like your website, mobile app, or connected TV application (i.e., Apple TV, Roku, etc.), or launched as standalone products. Technologists should be brought in to design these built experiences and products before they are sold. In fact, they should be included in (or drive) ideation cycles. The more you can create compelling products and experiences, the better for potential partners—and for your fans.

Creative Alignment

The "built if bought" approach to technology products involves ideation and proof of concept work designed to serve metrics that matter to partners and limits the exposure of fully building technology solutions in search of partners. When ideation and storytelling align with partner needs, you can ensure that the investment in the technology will be covered by the partnership.

Be cautious though; I've seen many organizations run into trouble because they don't have an understanding of what will be required to deliver the experience, so they can't properly value and price the partnership (more on that below).

Align the Experience with the Partner's Goals

To get the best results from partnerships, and ideally partners who want to sign again, spend the time to understand what matters to each partner. Sometimes an individual partner will want to be in front of as many fans as possible. Others want data, for example, in the form of a database of potential users. Still, others may want revenue or sign-ups for particular programs or products. When you know what the partner wants, design the program and delivery to provide that.

Years ago we built a gated content area with a premium offering for NASCAR as part of a partnership with a major telecommunications carrier. By reading the mobile device information on the way into the experience, we were able to allow the customers of the carrier to get access to the content for no fee, accruing value back to being a customer of the carrier and the partnership.

HOW TO CHOOSE A PARTNERSHIP TECHNOLOGY

Many technologies in the partnership space are custom built. Others may be assembled from pieces of open-source software, commercial Software as a Service (SaaS), or other technologies, and yet others may be bought outright from third parties. Use the same principles I discussed in chapters three and four to select technologies and to determine whether you will handle the given technology in house or outsource.

HOW TO SET PRICE

Pricing is probably one of the most elusive, critical aspects of partnership and also of partnerable technology design. The right price must be able to attract partners and ensure profit.

For most digital media experiences, the math is relatively straightforward. Let's say a leaderboard for golf gets 200 million page views per year. To determine price, divide those views by a thousand, and then multiply by whatever the industry standard CPM is at the time. Now, you know what the value of those impressions is, but you don't necessarily sell them that way.

When going to a partner to sell a package that includes media (i.e., ownership of a website section), the sale is a combination of art and science. For the science, do the traditional advertising math (views/CPM). The art is what the market will bear, the market's perception of the value of the positioning and placement beyond just the views. For example, you might tell a potential partner that the largest audiences for your motorsports property are on the leaderboard. If they want the leaderboard to be "presented by" their brand, that has value in excess of the media value. The packages may include placement like the one described above, some kind of bespoke execution (as in the NASCAR example above, accruing value back to being a customer of the carrier), plus signage and hospitality at the actual event. The holistic story around what the partnership represents beyond the assets and inventory *and* the story the partner can then tell the world is the value of the whole package. Again, the combination of art and science rules the day.

One important note. When delivering bespoke technology executions, which often have the most value to a potential partner—especially a technology partner—the price of the technology partnership must obviously be higher than the cost to build it, or the partnership will end up *costing* money. If you need to, get outside counsel with experience in the sports industry to help with design and pricing for these partnerable technologies. The right design and pricing will bring in major revenue for the organization, but the wrong pricing will cost you almost as much and potentially lead to angry partners.

THIS IS THE VALUE

Setting up the right expectations for partners and advertisers and delivering on them well are critical. The technology also *must* work. The higher the value of the partnership, the worse the impact from unmitigated breakages and the higher the stakes for good delivery become. But the juice is worth the squeeze: Creating partnerable technology can increase your budget and potentially fund everything else.

If you can come up with innovative technology concepts and build the stories required to fund them, you can add tremendous value to the organization. Fans will benefit, and so will your career.

As of this writing, most partners do not ask for granular metrics and data on whom their investment reached and, as a result, what the ROI for the partnership investment was. This is beginning to change, especially with partnership renewals (i.e., "Why should I do this again?") Your strategy should include the collection of data on your fans that can be used to deliver more tailored experiences and metrics that will prove critical to your partners. Over time, this practice will become more and more important to all your technology investments. Tailored experiences allow you to delight fans, bringing them into closer relationships with your sports property and delivering additional revenue through partnerships. When you use data strategically, you know who your fans are, how to give them what they want, and how to satisfy the evolving expectations of partners.

PARTNERSHIPS AND ADVERTISING: ACTION LIST

Apply the lessons of this chapter by considering the following:

- **Counsel.** Are you leveraging marketplace experience and intellect that can help guide what matters to big brands beyond traditional assets and inventory? If your internal team does not have this experience, do you have access to those who do?
- **Choice.** Run through a full audit of your assets and inventory. What inventory does your partnerships team focus on now? What is the pricing rationale? Is it attracting the partners you seek? Is there an addressable market of partners outside of the endemics in your space?
- **Governance.** Talk to your partnership sales team. How consultative is their sales process and how much do they understand how to sell custom and/or digital partnership products? Do they need additional training or support? Does their network include the types of brands that will make significant investments in your property? You may need some oversight of this team to ensure they are promoting these new offerings properly.

- **Execution.** Tech funded by partners *must* work. Ensure you have a clear idea of the level of effort to design, deploy, and operate partner-funded technology. Also, identify the gap between existing and aspirational target accounts and talk to them to understand what partnership vehicles and audiences they seek to reach. Design solutions that address specific business outcomes and show them how you'll measure success. Many partners may not yet be requesting those metrics, but this is where the market is moving.

7

FAN DATA AND MARKETING TECHNOLOGY

Major League Baseball is the most historic sports league in the world, with professional games dating back to the 1860s. Chris Marinak, the chief operations and strategy officer at MLB, recently explained, “From an outsider’s perspective, I think it’s easy to look at baseball as . . . conservative, consistent, at least when you look at the product on the field over a long period of time. But the reality is, behind the scenes, *innovation and technology are really at the heart of our business strategy.* That’s what is helping us propel the game forward . . . [and how we] create an active fan base over a long period of time.” MLB has created a consistent technology culture over decades, building and launching their self-contained app, their own ticketing platform, and streaming technology that Disney eventually bought for a total of $3.8

billion.* MLB has also invested heavily in technologies related to statistics and data, supporting both the on-field sport and the relationship with fans.

Data and statistics have always been hallmarks of baseball as a sport. Marinak says that this identity has driven MLB to use technology as a tool "to tell the story of the game [with stats and data]." He continued, "We did a lot of work with camera technology and utilizing other video technology to try to get the calls right on the field. And then that morphed into Statcast . . . We invested in player tracking, ball tracking, now bat tracking [to make more and better on-field data and statistics available for fans]."

MLB's data strategy goes significantly beyond the on-field data, however. The league as a whole plays over 4,800 MLB games in a season, with a devoted fan base who loves the experience of the ballpark. According to Marinak, the league and the teams collect the data they get from the in-person events and use it strategically, to build relationships with fans: "We try to build a portfolio of who our fans are. We have a massive database of almost 50 million people . . . that did something with us over the course of the last year. Bought a ticket, went to a game, got an email, signed up for a subscription." The amount of data that MLB and teams are able to collect is on par with banks, airlines, and other major corporations. The difference is that fans are often eager to hear from the baseball clubs they love and are more likely to spend money on additional experiences if properly positioned.

---

* Spangler, Todd. 2022. "Disney BAMTech Buys Out MLB Stake for $900 million." *Variety*, November 30, 2022. https://variety.com/2022/digital/news/disney-bamtech-buys-out-mlb-stake-900-million-1235444801/.

Data is at the heart of MLB's business strategy, both on and off the field. It means they're able to create better and more targeted experiences and better fan relationships. "It's how we reach younger fans, how we continue to connect with younger people and create an active fan base over a long period of time . . . The starting point is the idea of a first-party relationship with the fan." Rather than just collecting data and having it sit, MLB turns fan data into business intelligence, and opportunities to delight fans.

Their approach to data moves the sport and the league forward. Yours should do the same.

DATA IS THE FOUNDATION

Currently, the media landscape is being disrupted. The old broadcast media relationships that stood between a sports organization and the majority of their fans are attenuating or disappearing altogether. For many teams in North America, the substantial guarantees they've enjoyed in local/regional media rights are going away. While they should hold onto these guaranteed media rights deals as long as they can to survive and thrive, they must develop direct relationships with their fans. All sports organizations must shift to creating direct fan relationships through technology. MLB and the NBA (see chapter one) are two great examples of organizations that do this already, turning data into closer fan relationships and more control over their own revenue streams.

The key is data. When you have a strategic means to collect and use data, you know your fans on a deeper level. You can effectively create new products and services for those fans. You can offer them media experiences, like gated access to player stories focused on culture (i.e., describing the sneakers, music, or other things they love). You can invite fans to a bobblehead day for their favorite player. You can get more revenue out of the same fans, while creating additional value for them.

Organizations who can turn data into direct relationships earn fan loyalty at a level never before possible. They may also eventually be able to replace a portion of the revenue that their regional media rights deals used to provide.

THE FAN CONTINUUM

In the sports industry the concept of a fan continuum has existed for many years and is used to describe the types of fan personas. On one end of the continuum, "emerging fans" include subcategories of "unaware," "curious," and "casual." This type of fan occasionally glances at scores or occasionally watches a game digitally, via broadcast, but rarely attends in person. They care about the sport and/or the team, but it does not take up a large place in their lives. In the middle are "engaged" fans whose subcategories include "informed," "committed," and "passionate supporters."

At the other end of the continuum, "core sports enthusiasts" include actual "participants" of the sport, "avid fans," "evangelists/ambassadors," and "lifetime enthusiasts." These core sports enthusiasts care deeply, and the sport and/or the team represent a very large place in their lives. They attend many games/races/matches, buy merchandise, and follow extensive editorial coverage of the team and players. They eagerly participate in fan experiences and are members of some sort of loyalty program, providing important data to sports marketers. Avid fans connect with the sports property deeply and are happy to spend money to do so.

Of course, there are also many steps in between. One of the most important jobs for any sports marketing executive is to progress fans through the continuum from "emerging fans" to "core sports enthusiasts."

SPORTS MARKETING BASICS

The purpose of marketing technology is to drive the primary outcomes that all marketing execs are focused on: (1) increasing acquisition/retention, (2) reducing acquisition costs, and (3) driving a greater share of wallet. Our experience with leading sports organizations reveals a consistent pattern: 40 to 50 percent of marketing budgets unintentionally go toward fans with low conversion potential, while high-value segments remain underinvested.

Sports organizations don't just seek new fans but often prefer to look to deepen relationships with existing fans. If the organization can offer existing fans better experiences, they may be able to increase revenue at a much higher and more sustainable rate than they would by simply attracting new fans. (Getting new fans can be expensive, and their initial engagement can be small; delighting existing fans and deepening relationships often costs less and yields more.) In sports marketing, the Pareto principle, also known as the 80/20 rule, always applies. Put simply, the rule states that 80 percent of outcomes are the result of 20 percent of causes, or, in sports marketing terms, 80 percent of your future revenue will come from 20 percent of your fans. The question is, do you know who that 20 percent is?

Another View on Marketing

Shripal Shah is an extraordinarily experienced executive in sports. He teaches sports marketing for the master's program at Georgetown

University, and, in a past life, he was SVP, chief strategy officer with the Washington Commanders and CDO at Catalyst (part of Endeavor Global Marketing). Shah has led major sports properties to achieve significant digital revenue growth while generating hundreds of millions in revenue. Today he works with us as our chief digital officer, and I asked him about his basic philosophies around marketing and marketing technology.

"I think as much about missed opportunities as wins. Every time a potential avid fan (VIP) receives a generic, untargeted message, it's more than a missed sale—it actively reduces their future lifetime value," he said. "The right data-driven engagement strategy can make the difference between a one-off purchase and a long-term relationship that fuels your revenue growth."

How can you offer avid fans more targeted opportunities to buy? For example, you might send a fan an email on their birthday with two free tickets. When a popular player's bobblehead event comes up, you might prompt people who've marked that player as their favorite to buy discounted tickets to the event. Engaging and retaining fans with data means creating experiences for them using what you know about their likes and preferences.

The NBA Uses Data for Personalization

Remember our discussion of the NBA from chapter one? They use fan data to personalize their app with each person's interests and preferred formats. Here's the quote from Chris Benyarko, NBA, again: "Some people still like to look at traditional two-and-a-half-to-three-minute highlights. And other people want to just swipe through vertical video . . . One of the advantages of having a digital delivery is that you can present the game in almost endless amounts of ways. So you can have different camera angles, different audio . . . different languages, but also how you call the game . . . adding a pop culture element, [or] some of the heavy stat-based stuff." This effective use of personalization means building and appending profiles both implicitly and explicitly. The result is that over time, fans become more engaged with content longer, and more frequently.

The NBA translates its investment in technology and a direct relationship with fans into long-term opportunities for additional revenue. Knowing their fans better allows them to offer fans more products and services they might be interested in and translates directly into more revenue long term.

Who you are as an organization should drive your decisions on fan engagement. What are your priorities, and how much can you invest in long-term fan relationships and loyalty? Larger businesses may have the resources to create detailed personalized experiences, as the NBA does. Smaller organizations may have to make strategic choices about how to best serve fans and the organization in the short term.

A Great Loyalty Program: Path to Incredible ROI?

A great loyalty program could quite possibly be a path to incredible ROI, but effective loyalty programs are very difficult to pull off.

In an article he wrote for his recurring column on AI-powered sports solutions called *The AI Playbook* for the sports site *JohnWall-Street*, Shah says, "Loyalty is viewed by sports properties as the ultimate prize. And that's with good reason. According to a Motista study, fans with an emotional connection to a brand have a 306% higher lifetime value (LTV) compared to those merely satisfied by it.[*] So, it makes sense that rights owners across the industry have implemented rewards programs meant to cultivate deeper bonds with their supporters."

And the data that backs this up doesn't stop there:

- Eighty-one percent of consumers are more likely to do business with a brand that has a good loyalty program, and 76 percent are more likely to recommend brands with good programs, according to *The Loyalty Report* published by Bond.[†]
- Eighty percent of companies that measured their loyalty program's ROI saw positive benefits, with the average being gains of 4.9x over expenses, the *Global Customer Loyalty Report 2023* reveals.[‡]
- Seventy percent of US consumers surveyed for the *US Consumer Trends Index 2023* said a brand's loyalty program is important or critically important to their

---

* T, Viraj. 2018. "Motista's Study Results Conclude That Emotional Connection Is the Key to Brand Success." *MarTech Series*. November 7, 2018. https://martechseries.com/sales-marketing/customer-experience-management/motistas-study-results-conclude-emotional-connection-key-brand-success/?utm_source=www.johnwallstreet.com&utm_medium=referral&utm_campaign=points-based-loyalty-programs-can-work-in-sports-with-tech-evolution.

† "The Loyalty Report™ 2024." n.d. https://www.bondbl.com/theloyaltyreport.

‡ Antavo. 2022. "Global Customer Loyalty Report 2023 | Antavo." Antavo. December 8, 2022. https://antavo.com/reports/global-customer-loyalty-report-2023/.

choice, and 66 percent of global consumers feel the same.*

Monetizing Fans

Once you have good relationships, you can use digital channels (such as email newsletters, app alerts, SMS, and so on) to drive more ticket sales and sales of other experiences. You can also turn visits to your digital properties into partnership and advertising revenue.

For example, Next League has built dozens of live-event experiences for leading sports organizations, where fans can watch highlights, see leaderboards, or read news stories on their site. Many of these platforms also show live video during the event. All these incremental pieces of the overall fan experience can be attached to partnerships. Depending on the scale and length of the event, platforms like this can generate millions of dollars per event in advertising alone, and often multiple millions in partnerships. Of course, to make that kind of money requires close relationships with a large number of fans.

DATA DRIVES CONVERSION

Fan data isn't free; it costs resources to collect, store, and manage. Having a mature data strategy helps ensure that costs are manageable and ROI is possible. The right execution may help to drive fan loyalty and experiences and generate new revenue streams.

---

* Marigold. 2024. "Discover the Global Consumer Trends Index 2024 | Marigold." June 26, 2024. https://meetmarigold.com/consumer-trends-index/.

The explicit request for data (more on this below) can be seen as a trade; fans will trade data for things like access to highlights, live events, or gamified experiences. When a user accepts this trade and performs the action the organization wants, we say the user *converts*. Key to the concept is the fact that not everyone who's asked to perform the action will; in even the best offers, with even the most engaged users, upward of 90 percent of users will not convert. That said, the difference between 5 percent and 10 percent conversion can mean significant revenue.

When it comes to conversion, the key is good data. The more we understand about a fan and their preferences, the better we can target messages that will convert—the fan is getting more of what they want and will click or buy more easily. If Amazon knows I browsed lawnmowers yesterday but did not buy one, they will serve me offers for lawnmowers today. The more you understand about an individual fan, the more likely it is that you can offer them something they want to buy.

THE WAYS WE GATHER DATA

Fans give sports organizations data in two ways: implicitly and explicitly. Fans may **explicitly** give you information such as their name, email address, and preferences as a trade for something you give to them, for example, additional content, features, or access. Fans will be less willing to give over explicit data if it gains them little in return.

Explicit data is a two-edged sword; it can strengthen or weaken a relationship with a fan, depending on how it is used. If a sports organization uses that data in a way that feels intrusive, fans will lose trust and disengage. Whereas if that data is used to offer the fan more tailored experiences and opportunities, they will tend to become more avid over time. Explicit data is not dependent on anything except the willingness of the fan to provide it.

Implicit data, in contrast, is collected from the actions and behavior that can be captured without the fan offering specific pieces of information. They may simply approve of the fact that you are "watching" based on the way that cookies, server-side tracking, etc. track their actions and activity. So, for example, if a fan visits a league's main web portal, that fan may be cookied and tracked as they interact with the site's content. In most cases, the tracking technology will also be able to record what other sites they've visited and how they have behaved on those sites, often including things like purchase history and geographic location. Again, the difference here, regardless of the specifics of the data gathered, is that the fan did not explicitly provide the data, they simply approved that the site could gather what was available.

Where the Data Comes From

While data can in theory come from anywhere, there tend to be a few sources of data that are most helpful for sports organizations:

- advertising (especially advertising tracking on your owned-and-operated properties)
- cookies
- logins and other information
- profiles created by fans
- loyalty programs that fans join
- past records of behavior, such as tickets or merchandise purchased while logged in
- social media and site visits

- information generated by social media tracking, when purchased (e.g., Facebook data)

The more that a sports organization can draw fans to their owned-and-operated website, app, or other technology product, the better. It is easier to gather data on platforms that a sports organization controls. Fans on owned-and-operated products can be monetized, and their behavior and other data points captured, more easily.

As discussed in the last chapter, changes in advertising and laws around the data that can be captured may also make data more difficult to gather over time.

WORKING WITH DATA LOOKS DIFFERENT FOR DIFFERENT ORGANIZATIONS

The smaller, more lightweight side of fan data is simple: It begins with a spreadsheet of email addresses from ticket purchases combined with an email marketing service like Mailchimp or Klaviyo. Nearly all commercial email newsletter providers now offer good segmentation and targeting, so keeping track of which people engage with what is straightforward. This lightweight approach can be quick, easy, and effective with a good digital marketer.

On the other end of the scale, the largest organizations may need to invest in data scientists, marketing executives, business intelligence people, as well as the conversion and digital marketing specialists needed to get the most from the data. They will invest in people, processes, and technology to leverage data in a way that's most meaningful to the organization.

For many organizations, building data strategy and the technology to power it requires building a muscle around data and its collection, storage, and use. Just like software, your strategic approach to data management should be done iteratively. If very little exists, start with someone who understands digital marketing and how to begin to work with data. You'll eventually need someone to develop a data strategy who can help you build out the team and technology.

Personally Identifiable Information

Not all data will have personally identifiable information (PII) attached to it. Your website cookies, for example, might track the origin and behavior of individuals without recording their name or email address. Any people who log in, on the other hand, might have extensive PII, down to and including highly sensitive information like credit card numbers.

In general, the more information you have on individuals, the more targeted you'll be able to make offers and the more personalization is possible. Unfortunately, more isn't always better from a legal perspective. Extensive laws exist about the collection and storage of data, both in the US and, to an even stricter degree, in the EU.* Data storage of PII *must* be secure, and you must have a plan for security; mistakes can carry strong legal and financial repercussions.

One of the easiest ways to ensure that your organization complies with privacy and data storage laws is simply not to collect data with PII attached. Or choose not to collect or store certain

---

* As of this writing there are some early signs that regulators in the EU are concerned that overly regulating emerging technologies like artificial intelligence, and the EU AI Act specifically, may cause their countries to fall behind. More on that at symbio6.nl/en/blog/criticism-of-eu-ai-act.

kinds of data at all, for example, by outsourcing credit card processing to a trusted third-party transaction management system connected by API. You will then receive the funds but not the credit card number.

I recommend *being extremely thoughtful about all data, not just PII,* and then working to ensure compliance. If you are storing and/or managing PII, work with an established company that incorporates compliance and data security for you. Companies like OneTrust and BigID are examples of enterprise solutions that offer tools for GDPR (General Data Protection Regulation), CCPA (California Consumer Privacy Act), and other privacy regulations compliance.

A SMALL TEAM CAN DO A LOT

Technology enables more efficiency and effectiveness in sales and marketing than ever before. A small team—and in some cases, a single person—can drive revenue in ways that would have been impossible just two decades ago. For example, a single marketer can send out an email blast an hour before the game with an offer of a last-minute, reduced-price ticket with a hot dog for those who do not yet have tickets. That transaction would have been impossible in a world where paper tickets needed to be mailed. Even twenty years ago, sending out the email would have been more labor-intensive and much less targeted.

Today's technology also allows for A/B testing, permitting organizations to send out different versions of an offer (including things like tested, AI-generated subject lines) to similar segments, to see which version converts better. With creative thinking and careful testing, sports organizations can learn what their fans like on macro- and microlevels. They can test their way to more efficient ticketing flows and higher revenue.

FAN LOYALTY IS EARNED

If you provide fans with exceptional, tailored experiences, the data that you acquire from them will be considered a fair trade. If you don't uphold your end of the deal, though, you will lose fan trust and engagement. Loyalty is earned one relationship and one interaction at a time.

Keep in mind that data isn't inherently valuable and storing and managing it does incur cost. So, if you are to collect and store data, make sure you have a strategy that will both create great fan experiences and value *and* increase revenue. Make your fans feel seen and appreciated, and they'll reward you for it.

In the next chapter, I will show you how to approach technologies in the venue and in-person events.

DATA AND MARKETING TECHNOLOGY: ACTION LIST

Apply the lessons of this chapter by considering the following:

- **Counsel.** Does your organization have the internal expertise to develop a data- and customer-acquisition strategy? Does your team have perspective or experience with loyalty programs? If not, seek the expertise of someone who does.
- **Choice.** The technology required to deliver against your strategy also requires important decisions. Do you currently have CDP and CRM platforms that tightly

integrate to serve both marketing and sales? If not, run a cost/benefit analysis to consider how you may be able to get there. Create a plan for custom experiences: What are your options based on partner needs?

- **Governance.** Who's in charge of your data strategy? Your CTO? CMO? Do they also own the technology that's responsible for delivering against it? Where do data analytics, data science, and business intelligence report? Who owns and is responsible for the outcomes?
- **Execution.** Deploy a customer data strategy to aggregate and structure your data so it can work for you. What value do you offer your fan in exchange for data? Can you increase that value in order to acquire new fans and generate more revenue? **Make sure your data storage is legally compliant with data privacy laws.**

8

VENUE AND EVENTS

Katee LaPoff, the chief technology officer at Oak View Group (OVG), a company that provides operations, management, and/or hospitality services for over four hundred sports and entertainment venues, including new and visible properties attached to prominent sports teams around the world, explainss OVG's business model this way: "We have what we call our owned-and-operated venues, buildings that we literally put shovels in the ground and build from the ground up, and those we manage on behalf of others." For each venue, OVG uses a "matrix of thinking" to make technology "right sized," addressing the business and market requirements of each city.

OVG thinks of technology differently than the traditional tech world does. While tech, to them, includes venue internet access and digital ticketing, it goes beyond that to anything that creates a "frictionless experience" for fans or "enhances" a fan's end-to-end venue experience. LaPoff notes, "Technology, when it's foundationally at its very best, in venue context, it's about connecting an artist with their fan, a fan with their sports team."

LaPoff says that in a modern venue, technology enables everything "from buying a ticket to arriving in one of our venues . . . [and allowing fans to] tap your ticket and walk through a security screening process [as unobtrusively as possible, and then] interact with digital signage for wayfinding . . . get to the seat, get to the beverage offering of their choice." Safety and security technologies are also part of the venue experience.

OVG goes to great lengths to match technology to each venue. For example, they customize each point-of-sale experience for buying beverages and food to match "what [the fan is] used to outside the venue, tying in technology that [they] use inside your typical grocery store or big box retailer specific to the market they're in. What works in New York and what may be necessary for them is going to be very different than in Austin, Texas, or Palm Springs or Manchester or in Canada."

As LaPoff says, technology is "an enablement, not a purpose." The purpose, instead, is to make the experience of live entertainment in each venue as smooth and memorable as possible. "As good as the experience can be in your living room, there's not twenty thousand other people there with that same energy and that enthusiasm. There is just something so powerful about that. There's nothing like being there."

To attract and retain fans for in-person events, then, it becomes critical to provide experiences they can't get remotely. That means strategically choosing technologies that support the excitement of *being there.*

A CHANGING WORLD

Less than a hundred years ago, the only way to *see* a game, match, or race was to go in person. Remote consumption of sports content began with radio sports broadcasts, before we ushered in the era of television broadcasts of games when it became possible to watch sports at a distance. In the beginning, the quality of the picture wasn't great. In fact, in the late nineties, after acquiring rights to NHL games, Fox Sports was so concerned that people couldn't see the puck in the fast-paced games that they added a glowing trail to it. Fox Trax, as it was known, was an augmented reality system used to track the puck, and, as augmented reality went, it was way ahead of its time. It was also absolutely hated by NHL fans who found it gimmicky and a huge distraction. It was discontinued after the 1997–98 season. By 2010, nearly half of the TVs in America were high definition,* and even casual NHL fans could easily see the puck even without the glow. The improved quality also made it more comfortable to stay home to watch the game without missing anything. In a high-definition world where the game is easily seen and experienced on television, how do you get people to pay lots of money to go see games in person? Over the past few decades, billions of dollars in steel, concrete, and technology have been poured (literally and figuratively) into creating amazing venue experiences for fans to entice them to experience sports in person.

Sports executives have also shifted their focus to the behavior of the next generation of fans. It's been less than twenty years since the first iPhones rolled out (as of this writing), but mobile

* "9.1 the Evolution of Television | Media and Culture." n.d. https://courses.lumenlearning.com/suny-massmedia/chapter/9-1-the-evolution-of-television/.

technology has impacted both the way fans can experience sports and the way they interact with the world more broadly. They may or may not be interested in consuming a whole game at once, let alone committing a full day to go in person. How do you serve a generation of sports fans whose behavior will be radically different from any previous generation of fans?

From the perspective of executives like LaPoff, the answer is to offer experiences that only the venue can provide. What food is available at the stadium? Can it be ordered from the seat? What is the atmosphere in the building, and what is it like to be around tens of thousands of other sports fans? Venue technology has begun to reflect the need to provide new value in *being there.*

Take Me Out to the Ballgame

In-person games still provide unique value across sporting properties, as Major League Baseball emphasizes. As MLB's Chris Marinak says, "What we think is special about baseball as an entertainment entity, which is the in-person element . . . We have over a hundred million people that go to a major league or minor league professional baseball game every year. That's larger than *all the other major sports leagues combined.* And so we feel like that creates this first-party relationship with the fan over something that's oftentimes a person's most memorable experience. You're going to the ballpark with your family, with your friends. You're going to have this great experience outdoors in the middle of summer . . . And we have that relationship with you."

According to Marinak, MLB sees the in-person game to be a key component of their relationship with the fan. They use their app to both establish a good experience in person and to collect data to better serve fans going forward. The Ballpark app provides personalized ticket delivery and creates a seamless experience of entering the ballpark. "[During the game, the app] helps us reach our consumer, communicate information to them, and then get them to have a great experience [in person at the game]," Marinak said. Then, after the events, they use that same digital technology to set up access to unique experiences such as access to Hall of Famers, the All-Star game, and autograph sessions, to build fan relationships on an ongoing basis. MLB knows who their fans are, supports them in the venue, and invites them back to other experiences. But the in-person games connect the fan with the emotional bond to the teams and contribute to building the relationship moving forward.

MOBILE MAKES IT PERSONAL

Creating experiences that are better—or different—for the fan often involves a venue-compatible app. Technology can allow for easier ingress and egress of fans to the game, provide easier parking, and give personalized on-location content. It can offer free upgrades to loyal fans first. It can create games for fans to play during downtime.

Since the goal is to create new and different experiences for fans that they cannot get at home, some executives choose not to create certain app features, calling those features distractions from the in-person experience. For example, I have heard sports executives say publicly that they don't actually want rich mobile experiences. They want the fans in attendance to be watching the court/field/ice/track and not staring at their phones the whole time. When fans are very engaged, that's better for teams. They're right, of course, but human behavior is what it is.

If you've ever been to an international football match, like a Premier League match in England, thousands of fans are all watching the pitch—from the start of the match to the finish—riveted by every pass, shot, and tackle. Every fan is in their seat for the start of the match and back in their seat after halftime, for the entire ninety minutes of play. I've experienced international football matches in a few different European countries, and this has been true no matter where I went. Conversely, I have never been to a game—in any sport—in the US where every single fan is focused on the game action the entire game. (The only similar experience I've had in North America was in the old Forum in Montreal for a Canadiens game, where fans watched every minute of play.)

Incidentally, the opposite experience can be just as powerful. Tailgating with other fans is a huge part of the experience for NASCAR races; it is a cultural event, where the excitement and the human connection become the point. NASCAR actively encourages these experiences, allowing fans to bring coolers and food with them. They structure their technology to give fans something to talk about at races. The same is true in the parking lots at NFL stadiums.

What experiences can your venue offer that are different from seeing the game or match at home? Which ones can be enhanced by technology?

SATISFYING MORE THAN ONE GROUP

Venue technology is unique for two reasons: (1) "In-person" necessitates hardware and physical delivery, and (2) venues are required to serve *many* sets of needs. I'll start with the second.

Most venues not only host sports teams but also other performances and events. LaPoff says that technology at OVG's venues must be used by the "many constituents that live in a venue," including the anchor teams, the vendor partners—food, beverage, hospitality, ticketing, janitorial services, and so on—the tour and production companies, as well as the sporting events, artists, and teams. "And then you have your guests, your employees; all of those consume technology in very different ways. You have this environment where you have all of these divergent needs with still limited budgets, limited staffing."

Even when a venue does not have to host performances, venues, like sprawling golf courses for the PGA TOUR or the LPGA and three-mile tracks for NASCAR, carry with them their own unique technology challenges for in-person events. The sports organization, the athletes, and the venue personnel likely all need different things.

The competing needs of several groups make technology decisions more challenging, especially in a world where technology groups must reprioritize on the fly. Yet, delivering venue technology successfully results in positive experiences across the venue's ecosystem, making fans, artists, and teams alike happy.

Which groups do your venue technology need to address and satisfy? What are their needs? What are the priorities for your technology, and why?

MORE ISN'T ALWAYS BETTER

To get the most out of your technology spend for venues, you may need to deliberately downsize or reuse existing resources, what LaPoff at OVG calls "right sizing" technology. LaPoff says, "We don't want to put infrastructure to a building just to have it . . . We really have to think about that twice." This approach also serves as a highly effective cost-control measure for organizations, as every dollar not spent represents better profits and better opportunities.

It stands in stark contrast to older thinking about venue technology. In reference to the time she entered the industry, LaPoff said, "you would hear things commonly like, 'put all the fiber that you think you need, double it and double it again. If you think you need a hundred data ports, put in a thousand just in case.' A colleague and I called it the 'one more brick' theory. 'I'll have what that guy's having plus one more brick.'" But the "one more brick" theory was unwieldy, expensive, and turned out not to have served its purpose long term.

Early in her career, LaPoff looked into how venue technology was actually being used years after builds: "I went back and interviewed a lot of people who built buildings in that era . . . colleagues in the industry that had some very large, highly publicized properties being built, and said, 'What did you have enough of? Not enough of? What do you wish you had done differently?' . . . And the things that I learned were a little shocking. That theory of 'just in case' didn't really bear out the way we thought it would. So now, every time we finish a new building at OVG, we look at that same set of questions: What did we do well? What did we not do well? What are we using? What do we think we wish we had done differently? And we call that whole process right sizing. We want to do the right tech for the right business purpose in the right conditions for the right community purpose." The approach not only allows OVG to ensure that the technology that's built will actually be used, but it also drives savings to their bottom line.

As you consider your own venue technology, use the right-sizing approach. Don't spend money on infrastructure or technology "just in case." Match technology investment with the local need and character—again, what might be right in New York may be wrong in Austin.

A GUIDE TO VENUE TECHNOLOGIES

Here is a quick guide to the major categories of venue technology. It is by no means exhaustive and takes only a tertiary look at several complex areas of technology in order to simply highlight that complexity.

Scoreboards and Hardware

What I'm calling scoreboards comprise not only the screens used to display scores but also the media technology in the building. A scoreboard is one of the best ways to reach everyone attending the game: For hockey or basketball, that's usually eighteen to twenty-three *thousand* people all tuned in to a single message. Scoreboards provide a home for public service announcements. They host advertising in addition to the signage around the venue. Do not neglect this advertising opportunity in your partnership agreements and don't forget the value of having partners provide funds for compelling scoreboard content.

Adding in-person content that you cannot get outside of the venue is highly beneficial to the fan experience. So is a basic level of high-definition picture, large screen, minimal glare, and long-lasting hardware. Spend the time to ensure that hardware is up to expectations and then consider how to use content on the screens to help enhance the fan experience beyond that. Compelling content about players engages fans in between the action. So do the interesting trivia games, fake races tied to fan votes, and other small moments that enhance the fan's experience. What else can engage people?

Hardware Investments are Hard to Upgrade

Unlike software-only technology, upgrading a physical screen or next-gen scoreboard can't be done with the push of a button. LaPoff says, "When you're putting in digital displays, large-format scoreboards or ribbon boards, when you're building a building from scratch, you can build that space in. There's a lot of base building structure that our guests and even tenant partners never see that is required to make that center hung from the ceiling and the ribbon boards be on the face of the bowl seating infrastructure."

LaPoff says that both new builds and renovations bring unique challenges and frustrations with them: "When you have a renovation of a building, you have to deal with what's there, not what you wish was there. There's not one better thing or the other. Sometimes when you have all the choices in the world, it can be overwhelming and you can go off into an interesting design spiral. Sometimes when you're in a fixed environment, you think, these are the things I have to deal with, let's deal with it. There's not always one better than the other. But I will say from a sustainability perspective, we think long and hard about tearing things down before we build something new."

What specific challenges does your venue's space bring? What technologies will you need to plan around versus which can you build from scratch? How do these technologies influence the fan's experience? What technology can you reuse to preserve funds for other investments?

Merchandise and Point-of-Sales Technology

Food and beverage and merchandising providers all work with the venue to leverage third-party point-of-sale (POS) systems. Some vendors come to the table with their own proprietary solution, but most customize enterprise-level POS platforms that already exist. Up-and-coming technologies in the merchandising and POS space include the "just walk out" purchasing technology being tested by Amazon,* and the ability to use biometrics to pay. Biometrics use some form of physical marker—like facial recognition or a thumbprint—to identify people and allow the purchase to be charged to the correct person's credit card or other account.

Access Technologies

When it comes to access control (i.e., authentication for getting into the building), there are systems for barcode scanning on physical tickets and/or mobile apps, RFID for contactless entry (again, often via mobile app), and biometric-identity access management like facial recognition. There are companies like Fortress who offer comprehensive access-control solutions that include ticket scanning as part of a larger security and crowd-management system. (One of the advantages to this approach is the quality of the data you can gather and aggregate.) Just like biometrics can be used to identify people in the merchandising space, the technology can also be used to make entrance to the venue smooth. Facial recognition significantly increases the velocity at which people enter a facility and helps to identify security risks sooner. It can ensure that only authorized people are able to access secure areas and allow for changes to those authorizations at will.

---

* Recent press seems to indicate that Amazon is decreasing investment in this technology, as it may not have provided the results they wanted. I recommend being cautious and creating a test case before investing widely.

Technology also makes access within public areas of venues easier. Cameras and tracking technology can allow fans with an app to identify which gates, bathrooms, or concession stands have the shortest lines to make the venue more efficient at serving large numbers of people. They can identify parking, enable paperless tickets, and allow for those tickets to be transferred and redeemed seamlessly.

Lastly, compliance and accessibility technologies ensure that access to information and facilities considers everyone regardless of visual, hearing, mobility, or cognitive impairments. When serving the public in large numbers, this technology becomes more important than ever, both to identify people who need extra assistance and to provide that assistance with automation.

The Venue Ecosystem

There are dozens and dozens of vendors who each represent a piece of a complex venue ecosystem. This ecosystem manages everything from your ability to purchase and validate parking to accessing the venue via a valid ticket, purchasing a beer or hotdog, etc. Managing the venue ecosystem means having staff and partners who understand the complexities of the dependencies that exist between the systems, processes, and protocols for when things don't work as expected and, even more importantly for a venue, what to do in the case of an emergency.

Connectivity

Fans expect connectivity throughout a sports venue in the same way they expect it everywhere in their lives. It used to be that a large cellular provider company would partner for the entire stadium, for example, the AT&T Stadium for the Dallas Cowboys, and would put in the infrastructure. Then, special experiences could be designed for fans who got their cell phone service through that provider. In some historical cases, fans who got their service from competing companies might have their data slowed down, but that doesn't happen much anymore.

Now, venues often contract with what are called neutral host providers, companies who set up hardware and connectivity that is compatible with all providers. Neutral host providers set up the technology stacks and then are responsible for maintaining it.

In the case of Wi-Fi, the networks are designed to support, in some cases, over one hundred thousand people all online at once, but with varying degrees of success. People have said that the upcoming 6G technology may be able to replace the need for Wi-Fi in stadiums, but we'll have to see. The same thing was said for 5G. The reality is that providing high-speed cellular connections that serve tens of thousands of people concurrently in a relatively small space is not an easy problem to solve. But the technology is improving.

Sports Are Not Standard Events

John Martin at NASCAR recently told me a story about hiring a large telecom partner to install Wi-Fi for one of their massive tracks. He described sending the company a schematic: "They look at one section. They extrapolate out how they would install it. And they give us a price." NASCAR reminded the vendor that they have grandstands distributed throughout the schematic and that the environment will be different across the venue. The telecom company acknowledged the new information and said they would extrapolate it out. Martin continued, "Okay, everything's great at this point. We're locked in on this price. They came back out and they were like . . . wait, those grandstands are different than those . . . So I don't think they understood based on their stick-and-ball sport experience that these were each built in a different decade in a different style. And you're going to have four different installations in just one facility." The company finally came back and said, "Okay, we've learned our NASCAR lesson. We're not going to do that again." Martin laughed when looking back, but the stress at the time was real.

Be cautious about hiring and communicating with potential service and technology providers who are setting up connectivity hardware for a venue. Ensure that they truly understand the unique challenges of *your* sport and venue to avoid a situation like that one.

Ticketing

Sports organizations have options when it comes to ticketing technologies, but all involve third-party technologies. They can choose to integrate with a ticketing platform and handle ticketing themselves or redirect requests to a partner and have transactions take place off platform. Big leagues tend to have third-party partnerships that can manage transactions externally due to the tremendous volume and complexity of dealing with large events. Fans tend to already have accounts with the largest ticketing providers, so the experience can feel frictionless to them.

Ticketing providers typically offer two main integration options:

1. **Seamless integration.** Some providers offer APIs and SDKs that allow organizations to embed ticketing functionality directly into their websites and mobile

apps. This approach provides a more cohesive user experience, as fans can complete their purchases without leaving the organization's platform.

2. **Redirect model.** Other providers require fans to be redirected to the ticketing company's website to complete their transaction. In this case, the ticketing company manages the entire process, including inventory control and order fulfillment, ensuring customers receive their tickets.

Both approaches have their advantages, and organizations should thoughtfully evaluate which option aligns best with their financial model and technical capabilities. The seamless integration method typically delivers a smoother user experience but often demands greater development effort up front, and more maintenance later. On the other hand, the redirect model, while potentially technically challenging, is usually easier to implement but may present a clunkier user experience.

Other Ticketing Technology

Not every organization goes with a third-party provider, but the investment in managing your own ticketing technology is not insignificant. MLB has built out Tickets.com for their teams and to support other sports organizations. They obviously had the scale and technical aptitude to build out that model, but their solution is uncommon.

Mobile Apps

An app is a significant investment, both in terms of immediate outlay and in terms of maintaining multiple codebases. In most cases, a mobile app must be not only profitable but also a positive force on the fan experience to justify the work to build it. There are certain product companies that have created sports team and venue apps with a "greatest common denominator" approach designed to lower both capital and operational costs, but many teams and venues want something unique to them. Any app that is built should have a clear business case and a clear path to at least enough revenue generation to pay for its costs. (Normally through partnerships and advertising deals.)

The largest advantage of apps is that they can become a single point of control for things like access (ticketing), sales (food & bev, merchandise, etc.), and fan experiences (score, highlights, etc.) and that they can "maintain state." When someone opens an app, they have already validated and authenticated themselves through the phone's OS, and the sports app knows who they are. In some cases, the app can record what else the fan is doing on the phone whether the app is open or not. This provides a rich source of data to create individualized profiles. Buying a ticket becomes seamless, and offering loyal fans additional opportunities becomes easy.

Apps can host digital tickets for venue entry and display up-to-the-minute information on the shortest path to the bathrooms or concessions and which has the shortest lines. It can offer discounts on merchandise within the venue or the ability to order food or beverages from the seats. As a note, providing this kind of functionality can require integrating the app with other systems so that the provider receives things like orders or discount codes and can respond in a timely fashion. These integrations can be somewhat tricky to implement, so be sure to work with a software company who has done this exact work before to avoid costly delays and frustrations. In contrast, integrations with ticketing providers are often more straightforward due to well-tested and -maintained APIs, so if your team has experience with integrations, your organization may be able to handle those yourself.

And lastly, apps *can* provide the opportunity to personalize individual fan preferences. Or they can offer additional experiences. A few years back we built out The Fifth Stand, a Chelsea FC (UK) native mobile app, which provided things like a map where you can view local pubs in every country where Chelsea fans gather. The intent of this app was not to simply duplicate what was on the website but to leverage something that mobile phones are great at (i.e., geolocation) and create a rewarding experience for Chelsea fans around the globe who fancied a pint with other fans of The Blues.

As a note, if you can design a great experience for a fan, most commonly you will be able to find a partner happy to pay for that experience. But since additional features and capabilities cost more and take up additional time to support, leaders should consider the cost-benefit carefully when making decisions.

Where Venue Tech Is Going

The next wave of in-venue technology is to achieve the "golden record," or a 360-degree view of the fan, meaning the fan has the mobile app, and the organization knows when they're on their way to the stadium. Then, they check in at security to buy a parking pass, park their car, and scan their ticket in the app at the gate. Then, they stop and buy a hot dog on a system that's been integrated centrally. At every stage, the organization will know it's them, and the organization's CDP will be managing the data associated with each of their activities.

Right now, every step of that process is run by separate companies, and most of the time no "pure" 360-degree view of the fan exists in the venue. That said, it's possible, and it's coming. At Next League we invest a good amount of time exploring ways to acquire data and build bridges between sources of data so that organizations know more about fans. The existing ecosystem is complex, and the problem is big and complicated, but solving it will provide immense value to organizations. I predict this kind of integration will be the next frontier in venue tech (and may even be solved by the time you read this!).

EXPERIENCE IS KING

As MLB has said, the venue experience can provide a solid foundation for long-term fan relationships, if handled well. So, in a world where remote media experiences continue to improve, it becomes more critical to create meaningful experiences for fans in person. Providing value to the fan makes it worthwhile for them to come to the game.

In the next chapter, I discuss the power of media experiences that can be created outside the venue. Some feel that continuing to enhance these experiences for fans away from the venue may cause a drop-off in attendance, but I disagree. If there's one thing we've learned from massive technology disruption in this space, it's that fandom is not a zero-sum game. New experiences are additive. That said, the investment required to leverage technology to create meaningful fan experiences is not cheap. Finding a balance in how to invest, which experiences to create, and how to operate them efficiently will require a thoughtful set of highly strategic decisions. Some of those decisions are based largely in culture.

Where does your organization need to invest, based on who you are and where you are? What is the priority spend, and what can give you the most value for fans?

VENUE TECHNOLOGIES: ACTION LIST

Apply the lessons of this chapter by considering the following actions:

- **Counsel.** Where does counsel surrounding the tech in your venue exist? For some, it's the most senior technologist for a team; for others, it's specific to the venue business itself or in some outside counsel. Consider your strategy and philosophy about the way you will deploy venue technologies. For example, how will you ensure your technology addresses the business and market requirements of the city you are operating within? Does that philosophy start with the fan and work its way back to software, systems, and hardware?
- **Choice.** Don't just add "one more brick." How will you make technology "right sized"? Is sustainability a priority? Consider where you can reuse hardware and other venue technologies, where you can decrease scope to remove "just in case" purchases, and which physical investments will make the most impact on the fan experience. Consider the decisions around software/systems (and specifically data management) as early in the process as possible. The "golden record" is possible,

if approached properly, especially with venues that are under construction where not all the technology has been selected yet.

- **Governance.** Does the team responsible for physical architecture have the requisite experience to select the software and systems for your venue? Are you taking a program management approach to gain a holistic view of the way your venue tech will integrate? Who will ultimately be responsible for the operations and maintenance of your venue technology?
- **Execution.** If the team associated with strategy has put the fan experience first, what tools and metrics will you use to measure progress and status? Individual software vendors will think first about their own timelines and responsibilities—are you monitoring the overall program and jumping in to manage risk early enough in the process?

9

MEDIA TECH

I recently sat down with my close friend and business colleague Doug Perlman, the CEO of Sports Media Advisors, a man who is uniquely positioned to understand how media rights in the sports industry have changed from the mid-nineties to now and how technology has played a part.

Perlman was there for the beginning of the sports digital media rights revolution. He joined the NHL as a young lawyer and in the mid-nineties, volunteered to head up one of the first significant digital media rights deals in the industry. He jokes, "Had they realized how big a business it would be, they never would have let me anywhere near it . . . but it was brand new." He spent ten years at the NHL, eventually running the league's TV and digital programs and the NHL network, before moving to serve as president of IMG Media and then founding Sports Media Advisors. "We've worked with everyone from bowling and bass fishing and pickleball to the NFL and NASCAR and US Open Tennis." So he's seen a wide breadth of sports properties throughout a long history of media rights.

A few years ago, Perlman would say that "90 percent of the conversation is about technology, but 90 percent of the money is in TV." I asked him about this principle now that technology and streaming companies are coming into the sports media space. Does he still see people spending most of the time discussing technology and the future rather than the bread-and-butter media rights deals? "The vast majority of these deals are still about the live game rights and the current distribution methods for delivering those live games. That's where the money is, whether it's a traditional broadcast deal or a digital deal with an Amazon or an Apple. But so much of the conversation is still about the future. Nobody wants to make a mistake and sell a right too cheaply or not acquire a right . . . So even though you can agree on the big dollar number that's reported in the press and the core of rights that are being sold in the live games, you still have pages and pages of trying to future-proof the deals."

Perlman described the questions that are most concerning sports organizations now: "The world is changing and everyone's cutting the cord. The rise of direct-to-consumer and social and gambling and AI—what does it mean as sports properties look to distribute and monetize their content?" The problems are real, and in his words, interesting. "The valuation exercise has become more complex" as the tech streamers have entered the space and as sports properties like NASCAR and the PGA TOUR have developed the ability to produce their own content.

Perlman continued: "A major trend since I entered this business is that sports properties have become media companies in and of themselves and what that means has evolved. As soon as they got online with NFL.com or NHL.com, etc., they got into the media business. So that manifests itself in a lot of ways . . . It changes the dynamic in those negotiations significantly because the leagues and other sports properties are generally selling those live rights. But there's a lot of back and forth about what the properties can do. Can they offer alternate angles or alternate programming even within the live broadcast? What can they do with highlights? What can they do on social? . . . It creates a new dynamic where the property can distribute their own live games . . . That expands the universe of potential bidders . . . You can tell the story the way you want it to be told. You can help build stars."

Media Is About Technology

Of course, to take control of their own story, sporting organizations have to build out new technology to support new content production. Much of that technology is unsexy backend infrastructure, the technically difficult nuts and bolts to support real-time video and low-latency data. From the video of the event to the editorial about the event, the highlights, and the recaps, technology plays a critical role in delivering content to the fan. It's complicated to pull off effectively, but it's critical that it works. That's what fans expect when they tune into a game, match, or race.

The media space in sports has been experiencing constant change for decades now, and that change is only accelerating. At the time of this writing, we are facing the massive disruption of regional and college sports media rights deals and the rise of women's sports as growth properties, all of which are causing uncertainty (and opportunity) in the industry. Not to mention the huge technological change in the past few years.

I've been around long enough in this industry to say a few things for sure: Technology will continue to play a critical role in sports. Revenue from media rights in whatever form will continue to fund a large part of our industry. And successful sports properties will continue to find ways to use media technology to create appealing experiences for fans.

Media tech delivers the experiences that make fans as passionate as they are about their sport. That's why media technology is so important: everything from highlights to streaming live games and the data that powers low- and zero-latency scores, stats, gambling, and other experiences that enhance games. These are the technologies that literally connect fans to the game.

THE FAN'S EXPERIENCE IS MOST IMPORTANT

Media tech allows sports organizations to reach exponentially more fans than can fit in a venue. The eyeballs on television translate directly into ad revenue for broadcasters and media rights money for sports organizations. The technologies that allow sports organizations to create and manage their own media are just as impactful.

Occasionally I have engineers or product managers come to me with cool ideas for technology they would like to launch on behalf of a client. My responses are always the same: How will it help the fan, serve the partners, or add revenue? As Chris Benyarko of the NBA says, "Sometimes you hear people just innovate for the sake of innovating, roll something out new just because it's new. But ultimately all of it should ladder up to something that makes it easier for a fan to be a fan."

Many Fan Constituencies

Fans are not a monolith—in fact, there may be several sets of fans interacting with your sports property differently from each other. For example, in golf, the over-sixty fan group primarily watches golf on television every weekend. Next, there's a middle generation of people who go to LPGA.com, PGATOUR.com, or apps to get their information. Sometimes they'll tune in on television. The Gen Z fans (born 1997–2010), on the other hand, may not go to dot-com sites or dedicated apps at all. They get the majority of their content through interactions with each other and social platforms. And no one yet knows how the fourth group (Gen Alpha, born 2010–2024) will behave as they get older. We do know it will look more like Gen Z than older generations.

The way technology evolves will both influence and respond to changes in fan behavior. Some behavioral changes will be a result of the availability of new technology, and some new technology will be developed in response to changes in fan behavior. It's a virtuous circle. For example, the development of smartphones radically changed the way humans behave, and as a response to those changes in behavior, hundreds of business sectors radically changed the way they did business (or died trying). Mobile banking and the ability to shop for and purchase goods and services online have had a massive impact on the global economy, based on the development of smartphone technology and the willingness/desire for people to change the way they live. As of this writing, the global rideshare market is around $150 billion.* This is a business that did not, and

* Zoting, Shivani. "Ride Sharing Market Size to Surpass USD 691.63 Billion by 2034," Precedence Research. January 10, 2025. https://www.precedenceresearch.com/ride-sharing-market.

could not, exist before smartphones. Conversely, smartphone cameras have destroyed the once-thriving camera industry. Worldwide camera shipments dropped by 84 percent between 2010 and 2018.* Depending on their age, many children will never know what a camera even is. Taking a picture is just a behavior now.

While different fans will interact with your property differently, all of them share one key expectation: Technology should just work. No matter how complicated it is, they want their experience to work without them having to think about it.

CHALLENGES WITH MEDIA TECH AS A WHOLE

Throughout the rest of the chapter, I will discuss the four most common applications of these media technologies for sports organizations today: media production, content delivery, direct-to-consumer (DTC) application, and sports betting. The vast majority of sports organizations will find their use cases included in these categories, and those who have additional needs can approach technology selection as described earlier in the book.

Before I jump into the common applications, however, I'll stop to discuss three challenges to implementing media tech in general. To begin with, the delivery of live video remains technically complicated.

Video Delivery Is Hard

Delivering video requires more bandwidth and more layers of technology than other types of content. There are hundreds of moving

---

* Richter, Felix. "How Smartphones Devastated the Camera Industry." World Economic Forum, September 23, 2019. Accessed April 1, 2025. https://www.weforum.org/stories/2019/09/impact-smartphones-had-camera-industry/.

parts and external dependencies, all of which have to go perfectly for streaming to work as fans expect. Delivering video *live* for millions of people and peaks in traffic during a three-hour window is exponentially harder still. The cloud infrastructure required is expensive and complex. The platform and software have to be architected properly, the system has to stand up to massive traffic spikes, and it is highly influenced by environmental factors. All of this technical complexity is also true to a lesser degree for audio.

The more complex the system and the more revenue that depends on it, the higher the impact of breakage. As mentioned previously, when delivery is mission critical and there is significant revenue riding on performance, the cost of an SRE investment is worthwhile to mitigate risk with larger organizations.

The Need for Complex Cloud Infrastructure

Sports media must be able to be served to potentially millions of fans simultaneously during event windows. Rather than trying to build the infrastructure required in house, nearly all sports organizations and media companies work with external cloud providers like AWS, Google Cloud, or Microsoft Azure. These cloud providers invest in the infrastructure to be able to spin up additional capacity as needed so that millions of fans can experience the content during peak times without committing the organization to that capacity forever.

However, working with a cloud provider at the bandwidth, loads, and complexity that sports media requires is not easy. Either engineers with extensive experience in cloud technologies or third-party vendors who have that experience are necessary to ensure these relationships go well.

Rights and Entitlements

As complicated as media technology can be, the rights and entitlements part of sports media may be even more complicated, and technology must help manage that complexity. In sports media, there are always conditions under which people are (or are not) allowed to consume content, especially game footage like highlights or live games. For example, in the US, large sports leagues are the primary "rightsholders," meaning they own the rights to the events they put on (games, races, etc.). They license some of those rights to other organizations and keep some for themselves. (Typically selling rights has more financial upside than trying to monetize them directly, but there are other reasons to retain rights.) Some of those licensees may have the right to broadcast the live game but not to rebroadcast, and others may have the ability to deliver, say, highlight content to fans around the world, but not deliver anything live. The rights landscape dictates the conditions under which any specific group can deliver games or content.

Entitlements dictate who can consume given content and under what conditions. So, for example, on a recent trip to London, I wanted to watch a show I've been following on a leading streaming service. Even though I pay for the service, in London it was "geoblocked" (restricted based on my geolocation). I could not access that specific show because of where I was, even though I had the right to watch it at home. Sports rights are likewise often sold by region, and so what users have access to is sometimes dictated by where they are. Entitlements may also be driven by account type or payment terms. Subscriptions are often created with tiers, allowing access to more content to those who purchase higher (and more expensive) tiers. Depending on the type of entitlement they have purchased, fans may not be able to access premium-tier content if they've paid for standard access, and they may not be able to access anything if they are traveling. Teams also have the right to deliver content within their home markets (usually defined as a certain-number-of-mile radius around their home venue), and they usually can deliver content as they see fit within their venue, outside of the media rights that have been sold. Again, it's complicated.

Rights and entitlements are governed by strictly enforced contracts and payment terms, and complex technology is required to ensure that terms are met. The technology that controls "who can access what" while ensuring the terms of media rights deals are respected requires experienced technology teams and, often, dozens of vendors who control individual pieces of the puzzle. The technology here, as always, serves the business and the fan.

Low- and Zero-Latency

Another challenge of media technology is latency. Latency is a delivery concept; if something is delivered with low latency, it takes only a short amount of time for it to be delivered from one place to another. Although zero latency is only theoretical—physical limitations in the transmission and processing of data make it impossible—in sports technology, we refer to instantaneous delivery and receipt (where there is no perceptible delay) as zero latency. If a score for the game only gets updated on an organization's website every five minutes, then the information arrives too late to matter for many fans. These days fans get alerts across multiple platforms on things like scores or match status.

Low- and zero-latency data is critically important for sports betting in particular. But betting is not the only reason to invest in low- and zero-latency data technologies. Data arriving in real time substantially improves the fan's experience of certain events. For example, NASCAR takes timing and scoring data from a car going two hundred miles an hour, processes it, and then makes that data available as feeds to be ingested by internal and external constituents (i.e., NASCAR MOBILE). NASCAR fans can use the data made available to NASCAR MOBILE to see things like a real-time leaderboard with enhanced data including fuel and tire condition; live telemetry data showing rpm, mph, brake, and throttle information; and more.

Other sports combine their subject matter expertise in their sport, with available low- and zero-latency data to create a wide variety of compelling fan experiences.

MEDIA PRODUCTION

Traditionally, sports organizations have sold media rights to broadcasters, and the broadcasters are responsible for capturing, editing, transmitting, and delivering most of that content to fans directly. As consumers have "cut the cord," and technology has evolved, many rightsholders have seen an opportunity to play a more prominent role in media production. The evolution from sports league to media business has actually been underway for many years.

Of the five largest North American sports leagues (NFL, NBA, MLB, NHL, and MLS), four have launched their own broadcast networks (MLS has a streaming partnership with Apple TV+), and many sports properties have made huge investments in new media production facilities. In 2024, NASCAR opened a $53 million, 58,000-square-foot media production facility in Concord, North Carolina. Similarly, in January 2025, the PGA TOUR launched

PGA TOUR Studios, a state-of-the-art, 165,000-square-foot media production facility that serves as the central hub for all PGA TOUR media operations. Over five thousand hours of PGA TOUR Live on ESPN+ and an extensive array of more than fifty original, social, and digital media platforms will be produced within this new facility.

A Changing Business Model

Since 2019, when Diamond Sports Group bought Fox Sports and its regional sports rights and financial guarantees, the challenges around the economics of the regional sports network (RSN) model have been front and center. The Diamond Sports deal included forty-two professional teams (including sixteen NBA teams, fourteen MLB teams, and twelve NHL teams), and the channels collectively generated $3.8 billion in 2018 across nearly 75 million subscribers.* Between the time the World Health Organization (WHO) declared COVID-19 a pandemic in March 2020 and February 2023, when Diamond Sports Group failed to make a $140 million interest payment, it was clear that the company was in trouble. By March 2023, Diamond Sports Group had declared Chapter 11 bankruptcy and legal negotiations with MLB, the NBA, and the NHL were underway as of this writing.

Although direct-to-consumer models can technically deliver the same content to fans, media rights experts agree that leagues and teams can't replace the guaranteed income provided by the RSN deals by simply providing a streaming direct-to-consumer option; in fact,

* Littleton, Cynthia. "Sinclair Clinches Disney-Regional Sports Networks Deal, Byron Allen Joins as Partner." *Variety*, May 3, 2019. https://variety.com/2019/tv/news/sinclair-disney-regional-sports-network-deal-1203204685/.

it wouldn't even be close. "The economics provided by the previous RSN commitments were simply too large to expect that they could be replaced by DTC options," explained Doug Perlman. "Although they were also fair to broadcasters when originally conceived, that is simply not a viable model in a world of cord-cutting."

How regional sports organizations and affected leagues respond is an open question. Direct-to-consumer (DTC) programs may be part of the answer for some, which I will discuss later in the chapter. Equally important, though, is the need to expand the potential pool for buyers of media rights and to find additional ways to build relationships with and monetize fans.

Host Broadcasting Capabilities

Many of the world's largest organizations use centralized media production already. Host Broadcast Services (HBS), a subsidiary of Infront Sports & Media (note: OMNIGON was purchased by Infront Sports & Media in 2016), was established in 1999 to centralize the production of television and radio signals for the 2002 and 2006 FIFA World Cups™. Since its inception, HBS has continued to refine its capabilities by integrating experienced staff from past FIFA World Cups with expertise from across the broadcast and digital media industry. The International Olympic Committee (IOC) was also an early adopter of centralized host broadcasting services with Olympic Broadcasting Services (OBS) in 2001.

The broadcast side of logistics for these global events is incredibly complex. For both the FIFA World Cup and the Olympic games, the rights are sold internationally and broadcasters from around the world need production capabilities across dozens of sports in venues located all around the host cities. In most cases, production facilities need to be created from scratch prior to the games and then removed afterward. The creation of OBS meant that much of that production became a centralized service, then leveraged by broadcasters from more than 110 countries.*

Media Production Means More Options

I expect that all larger rightsholders will continue to build out their media production capabilities and maintain control of the way their sports are represented to fans, which will continue to become more critical to long-term objectives and growth in their sports. Organizations who choose to build out their own media production capabilities not only give themselves control of their content but also make themselves more attractive to a larger universe of rights purchasers. After all, if you don't need media production capabilities, anyone with the proper funding who wants to reach sports fans can become a bidder for rights.

In a world where the old business model is changing, the ability to bring more purchasers to the table is increasingly valuable. So is the ability to create additional content for the web or direct-to-consumer products for additional revenue opportunities. Production technology is a major trend that looks to only be accelerating for sporting organizations in the future.

CONTENT AND PUBLISHING

Content delivery technology has quite a bit of overlap with production technology, in that it usually leverages the production output,

---

* Sports Video Group, July 2024 (https://www.sportsvideo.org/2024/07/17/paris-olympic-preview-inside-look-at-obs-plans-for-11000-of-games-coverage/).

but not all content is rich media like video or audio. Here I am mainly focusing on technologies that are *not* related to on-demand or live-streaming video/audio—for example, a consumer-facing site populated with articles, recorded videos, and audio commentary.

Content Creation

There are a variety of technology tools to create content, including audio, image, data, and video content creation tools. Often, a writer will create an article, recap, or editorial content directly into a content management system (CMS) or publishing system, but occasionally there are other content systems as well. There is also an automated component of content creation. Game stats used to be created by people sitting courtside and recording events by hand. Now, it's being amassed by cameras, sensors, and automated systems and reported automatically by publishing systems.

Content Publishing

CMSs exist to publish much of the content you see on the internet. CMS platforms allow content creators and editors to create pages, draft content, and then, for example, populate a photo gallery using drag-and-drop technology without having to code. Video management systems are similar, where editors can publish and tag videos to be consumed in the right format by the fan. New AI tools are taking over much of this content creation and leaving editors to manage or moderate what is queued for publishing.

DIRECT-TO-CONSUMER TECHNOLOGY

For direct-to-consumer (DTC) products, organizations must have a system that can support identity management, subscription management, a CMS, and usually a “gate” on the product that authenticates subscribers. These technologies can be built custom, or they can be assembled or purchased as commercial solutions.

While authentication and entitlement technology is most often used with logins to allow paid subscriptions, it can also be used to gate based on geography or mobile carrier, for example. Once the person is authenticated, the system must be capable of delivering the specific content they are entitled to. Identity management systems often interface with a content management system (CMS) or subscription management solution to make this happen. Getting the various technologies to interface properly requires time and care.

While DTC products are not the answer to decreased media revenue entirely, as Doug Perlman highlighted earlier in the chapter, they provide an invaluable opportunity to build direct relationships with fans and ideally to monetize them for revenue *in addition* to traditional digital rights or broadcast rights deals. The most engaged fans have an almost insatiable hunger for the details of the sport and are happy to pay for additional content and experiences.

One of the most effective uses of DTC content is what is referred to as “shoulder content,” content that does not conflict with existing broadcast rights. For example, Formula 1 created *Drive to Survive*, a reality television series that features the F1 teams and their drivers like reality TV stars. The stories of the people, their personalities, and their emotional journey weren’t covered by F1’s media rights deals, only the live races. Netflix was willing to pay a licensing fee to F1, and Box to Box Productions was paid to produce the show.

The PGA TOUR has *Full Swing*, a similar behind-the-scenes reality program, which is also produced by Box to Box and executive produced by Pro Shop Studios, in which the PGA TOUR is a minority investor. NASCAR's *Full Speed* shares a similar format and is produced for Netflix by Full Speed Entertainment, a new production partnership formed by NASCAR Studios and Words + Pictures. Again, the point is that these large sports rightsholders are progressively becoming more mature media businesses as their production capabilities increase, and they seek further control of the way their sports are presented to the world.

As you consider your own DTC offerings, if you have them or will build them, what assets do you have available to monetize in new ways? What shoulder content can you build? What personalization can you add to the content experience? Seeing the same content with an additional or unique focus can offer additional value—for example, giving an avid fan more footage of a specific athlete than was available via traditional broadcast.

HOW OTHER LEADERS DO IT

Here are three sports technology leaders on the role of DTC and where media tech is going in the near future:

> **Chris Benyarko, EVP, direct-to-consumer products, technology & operations, NBA:** "We support multiple teams in terms of their local DTC offerings directly within the NBA app . . . And I will say the people who have those local DTC offerings are more engaged and they watch longer, they use more of the interactive features. They consume more of the content than any of the other fans that we have."

Scott Gutterman, SVP, digital & broadcast technologies, PGA TOUR: "We will continue to see this decentralization of consumption happen around all media. People will consume media the way they want it, how they want it, on what they want at the time they want it. And I think that's a huge opportunity and a particular challenge . . . The opportunity is to bring more people into your sport . . . So if somebody wants to come to golf through a Topgolf or through TikTok or through PopStroke . . . or even just through fashion, that's what we want to provide people . . . The challenge is that as consumption decentralizes, you have to continue to become a content creator. So determining what is effective on what platforms and how you create that content and how much it costs to do is going to be a big challenge."

Chris Marinak, chief operations and strategy officer, MLB: "I think we're taking the approach that we want to have all options available to us. That's one of the benefits of us having control of our technology is that we're not beholden to the market. We always have an option of delivering these things ourselves. If something else emerges in the market that works really well and is great win-win for everybody, then sure, we can always lean more toward partners. But if that doesn't emerge, then we have a great stack in-house that we can use and tell the same story to our fans and create a great consumer experience that way as well."

SPORTS BETTING

As the internet evolved, the ability to bet on sports on a mobile phone evolved alongside it—at least in the UK and Europe. In most parts of the United States, sports gambling was illegal until recently, but it has seen significant growth and attention in the short time it's been available.

Sporting organizations do not handle betting directly. Instead, they contract with outside betting organizations that provide revenue in exchange for accurate, low- or zero-latency data. Since the current trend is toward microbetting, where a fan bets live on microactivity like balls and strikes (in baseball), the data must be highly detailed and accurate in real time.

Sports gambling makes organizations money, but it also drives more focused attention from fans. Doug Perlman said in our recent conversation, "I think the notion is that when someone has bet on something, they're far more inclined to watch it . . . So the sports that engender lots of interest from people who want to place these bets [have media rights that are] increasing in value." The data supports this. According to an Altman Solon survey of fourteen thousand respondents, "Betting significantly reinforces sports viewing time, fandom, and sports-related media consumption—regardless of the bettors' team or player preferences." *

---

* Altman Solon. "Sports Betting Gains Popularity, Changes the Industry," *Altman Solon Insights, Analysis: 2020 Sports & News Survey* (blog), April 2021. https://www.altmansolon.com/insights/sports-betting-content-consumption.

Gen Z, Gen Alpha, and the Influences of Sports Wagering

I have a son who just graduated from college, and I've seen him and his buddies use betting apps for very small transactions. He says it makes the game more engaging and more fun. "The generation that's coming up has a totally different view on betting," Perlman says.

"Years ago, I heard a media executive use this phrase, which is, we need to be concerned about people following sports, but not watching . . . And I think the commonly held belief is that younger people have short attention spans, which may or may not mean that they may not be inclined to watch a three-hour broadcast. The evolution of incredible technologies means that you're able to stay connected with the sport even if you don't dedicate those three hours, right? Obviously, you can get the highlights and best moments . . . You can follow the individual players and get their perspective . . . So you can be incredibly connected to a property and maybe never sit and watch a three-hour window. On the one hand, it's good that people are so connected to these sports because there's lots of ways to monetize that connectivity," Perlman says, but sports organizations still make the most money from traditional broadcast media rights. Everyone is keeping an eye on the next generation to see how they can best be reached.

ALL ABOUT THE FAN

Media technologies are at the heart of delivering the experiences that make fans passionate about sports. They're some of the most mature and most important technologies there are. So, when investing in media technologies, start first with the fan. Understand what all your fans look like, from most committed fans to aspirational, from youngest to oldest, or any other important demographic. What do they each need? How can you make their experience better with technology?

Once you know what the fan needs, then consider the commercial value of what you are creating. If it's good for the fan, most of the time, partners will want to be involved. Their revenue will make technologies possible that you would never have considered if you had started with your budget or started with a technology solution and only then looked for a problem.

Delivering content well is table stakes for connecting with the fans and for building relationships with the next generation of fans, the ones who don't yet know what they'll want or need. To deliver for those fans, organizations will need to experiment. So in the next chapter, I'll talk about what the future of sports technology might look like. Let's move to the cutting edge—and why you may or may not want to play on that edge.

MEDIA TECH: ACTION LIST

Apply the lessons of this chapter by considering the following actions:

- **Counsel.** As you consider the media rights landscape your organization is operating within, make sure you have two experts who can help navigate this critical area of sports tech. First, ensure you have someone who can give accurate information about what is and is not allowed contractually, and second, make sure your technology group can advise you on the correct path forward based on the rights you have. These two experts may have to interact to ensure correct technical contract compliance.

- **Choice.** Will your organization invest in production capabilities, and to what extent? What low- or zero-latency data is needed to support betting, and does your organization want to invest in that arena? What DTC products make sense for you, if any? What technology is available to maximize advertising? There are quite a few choices that your team will need to make across the spectrum of available media technologies.
- **Governance.** Who will be responsible for making sure that the technology delivers the media rights and user entitlements required and that revenue opportunities are maximized? How do you bridge the gap between marketing technology (fan acquisition, customer data platform, CRM, etc.) and media technology (AdTech, CMS, streaming, live stats data, etc.) What controls and approvals need to be in place?
- **Execution.** In media technology, it just has to work. What approach will you take in both properly architecting and operating your media technology? Ensure you have the proper processes and protocol for when there are issues and ideally enlist a formal SRE team. Consider iterative delivery and descoping as needed.

10

PROFESSIONAL PERSPECTIVES ON WHAT IS TO COME

After Disney acquired Fox Sports, Devin Poolman and many of his former colleagues were looking for what was next. A colleague of Devin's, ex-Fox Sports executive Jeb Terry, had an idea. Poolman recalls, "Jeb started sharing with Sheli [Reynolds] and myself a famous cell phone video of a prototype of an LED dome . . . With this new LED dome capability came the application of bringing sports to life in a shared environment. Is that crazy? And of course, yes, it was crazy . . . But it was the fun kind of crazy."

Poolman accepted the job and went on to become the chief product and technology officer at Cosm, a company that uses cutting-edge LED dome technology to create innovative, immersive "shared reality" experiences that put audiences right in the middle of the action.

According to Poolman, "The first thing that we did as a company, as Cosm, [was] to actually acquire the world's leading planetarium company, Evans & Sutherland . . . [A planetarium is] not just the incredible technology that went behind the scenes, but from an experience perspective . . . let's all of us travel together to space. Nobody has anything but fond memories of going to the planetarium growing up . . . what an impactful experience that is."

The company then acquired a subsidiary called Spitz, a company with an incredible history in computer graphics going back seventy-five years, and C 360, an immersive video technology company. Once they added live production and VR capability teams, Cosm's leadership had to stitch all the pieces together to deliver on their goal.

Years later, Cosm's experiences exist in their full glory, exactly as the team envisioned in the beginning—which is no easy feat. The company works not only with sports properties like the NFL, MLB, Premier League football, the College Football Playoff, and the UFC, but also entertainment brands like Cirque de Soleil and is poised to expand to new cities over the next few years.

Where Technology Brings Experience to Life

I was fortunate enough to experience Cosm in person in Dallas recently, and I was struck by how impressive it is. Cosm's experiences comprise massive LED domes and 8K to 10K media. If you've seen clips of them, they do not do it justice. You truly have to be there in person to feel the impact.

The Cosm experience is about more than just the technology, however. Their attention to detail is clear, from the bespoke camera setup at the original locations to the quality of the venue experience. Poolman notes, "A fundamental premise we have is that experience should not just be about the technology and execution of the technology . . . Yes, technology plays a role, but hopefully technology can disappear and everything comes to life. Say, the way we use what we call the 'cap and canopy' on the top to augment the video for live production. But I'd say it even comes down to the physical design of the venue with regards to the investments, and the focus we've had on the service, the quality of the food, our fan ambassadors who welcome you in, the quality of the seating experience." The experience of the entire venue feels like very, very high-end hospitality.

Poolman explains, "We as fans want to go to a place . . . [where sport and entertainment events] come to life, not just on that screen that is in front of you, but every touch of the experience. It's like walking into a ballpark or walking into a stadium or arena. It's not just about, how does the field look? It's how do the hallways feel? And the opportunity to have people spend time with us and that time be more than just the game itself. It's coming early, grabbing a drink, it's staying afterward, it's hanging out on the deck . . . and that was critical for us to include in the design and thought that went into how the building was laid out."

Based on what I saw in Dallas, Cosm has more than achieved its goals.

Next-Generation Technology

Cosm is an excellent example of a next-generation technology company already making an impact on the sports viewing experience. And it's also an example of a counterintuitive truth I've been promoting for years. The technology that is coming in the near future is not just about getting people to stare at their screens—in fact, it's about empowering them to *not* stare at their screens. In many cases, it's about applying existing technologies in new ways or using new technologies to open up new experiences for fans. Technology is most impactful when it enhances people's lives.

Of course, pulling off cutting-edge technology experiences is challenging and comes with a substantial amount of risk. Whether you play at the cutting edge becomes a strategic decision that should follow naturally from who you are as an organization.

Your innovation culture should drive your decisions on when and how to play with new technologies.

THE FUTURE IS OPAQUE

It's tough to make predictions, especially about the future.

—Yogi Berra

Periodically I get asked on panels, "What will the technology landscape look like in five years?" "What's the future of AI?" or some other question. The truth is that I don't know, because nobody knows. What will happen in the future beyond a year or two cannot be known with certainty, not even to the foremost experts in their field. The hubris that is often innate to sophisticated technologists drives the desire to project what will happen in the future, but those are only predictions.

Now, that said, there are trends that influence the way that we invest in and use technology, and those trends can shape the future that we jointly build—or not. In very recent memory, for example, technology executives were talking about NFTs and VR headsets, but none of these technologies have received wide enough adoption to substantially change the future, despite their promise. The early internet with the dot-com bubble, the smartphone, and the advent of social media also started small, but these technologies gained steam until they changed the sports industry and the world. Social media specifically became make or break for sports organizations, and everyone, young and old, had to learn or miss out.

No one knows what the next technology is, the one that will massively move the needle for the sports industry. Organizations talk about and invest in experimenting with up-and-coming technologies to avoid getting caught flat-footed. If the industry moves in a particular direction, and your organization is behind the curve, it may cost you opportunities. But you may also lose the money and time you spent on experimenting with less than mature technologies.

Should you play on the cutting edge? You may want to, if your culture supports it and you have the time and resources to spend. Being there first may position your organization to lead in the future and attract partnerships and new fan experiences with a halo of innovation. Innovation does carry with it unique problems, of course. Newer technology will behave less reliably, and consumer behavior is tough to predict. The real paradigm shifts in technology are driven when we convince users to change existing behaviors to adopt new technology. In his influential book *Crossing the Chasm*, Geoffrey A. Moore focuses on innovative, high-tech products and the gap or "chasm" that exists between early adopters and the mainstream market. According to Moore, "Our attitude toward technology adoption becomes significant—at least in a marketing sense—any time we are introduced to products that require us to change our current mode of behavior or to modify other products and services we rely on." Simply stated, consumers need to be ready for the value exchange that requests a change in behavior. Sometimes they are ready, and sometimes they are not. However you approach the topic of innovation, there are risks and there are benefits. Make decisions in accordance with who you are as an organization and your priorities.

MY ADVICE

Jeff Bezos has famously described a view of the future that I agree with wholeheartedly. He says, "I very frequently get the question, 'What's going to change in the next ten years?' And that is a very interesting question; it's a very common one. I almost never get the question, 'What's not going to change in the next ten years?' And I submit to you that the second question is actually the more important of the two—because you can build a business strategy around the things that are stable in time."* In the sports business, technology may change, media may change, and even the rules of the game may change over time. What does not change are the fans and the business essentials. It doesn't matter if the innovation is "cool"; without a clear way to improve the fan experience, the partner experience, revenue, or all three, new technologies are toys at best.

Spend time anticipating how technology can help transform the experience that your fans can have with your property and your brand. What is the impact now, and what could the experience of a given technology be for the fan? What the team at Cosm envisioned wasn't something the average fan could have imagined five

* Haden, Jeff. 2017. "20 Years Ago, Jeff Bezos Said This 1 Thing Separates People Who Achieve Lasting Success from Those Who Don't." *Inc Magazine*, November 6, 2017. Accessed December 30, 2024. https://www.inc.com/jeff-haden/20-years-ago-jeff-bezos-said-this-1-thing-separates-people-who-achieve-lasting-success-from-those-who-dont.html.

years ago, but early experiments showed promise. Taking the risk to be first is often worth it if the fan experience follows.

The same goes for the business essentials. Any investment in new technology needs to have a realistic path to benefit the business, even if only by attracting more excited partners or shaping the brand in a given direction. How could potential technology benefit the direction of the organization and its north star? If future technology will pull the organization away from its goals, do not spend resources to experiment or invest in it. *All* technology decisions, even ones made with up-and-coming technologies, should serve the organization's goals.

"What Are We Doing about This Technology?"

You've likely been there: Someone from the C suite bursts into your office and asks about a specific technology: "What are we doing with AI?" for example, or "What are we doing about NFTs?" The question doesn't necessarily mean that the technology is a good idea or that it has any value for the organization, only that the conversation around that tech has gone mainstream.

The temptation is to respond with *some* way that the organization can incorporate the technology and to add that work to the roadmap. Instead of agreeing reflexively to make this new technology happen, try mentioning the organization's priorities and your KPIs. Then explain if the tech in question doesn't fall within any of those priorities. Or, offer to add the thing to the list of innovation experiments, with the understanding that it may not be accomplished soon without adjusting priorities.

If, on the other hand, the technology seems poised to answer your organization's goals and your fan experience, explore it. Still be cautious and ask what other initiatives it should supplant; you can only fit five pounds of sugar in the five-pound bag, and it's better to involve key people in the prioritization decisions.

A RUNDOWN OF FUTURE TECHNOLOGIES

Any complete guide to up-and-coming technologies would run much longer than the entirety of this book, so I only included technologies that have three primary and practical use cases for our industry: (1) the virtual, augmented, and mixed reality technologies that move fans from staring at their phones to interacting with sports venues and each other, (2) optical tracking technology, which uses a combination of computer vision algorithms and high-speed cameras to capture real-time data that sports businesses can use to monetize data, and (3) generative artificial intelligence (GenAI).

Virtual Experiences (VR/AR/MR and Beyond)

Virtual, augmented, and mixed reality technologies have existed for a few years now, both in headset form, as with Meta Oculus, Meta AI Glasses, and the Apple Vision Pro, and in other formats, like the NASCAR experience, where the fan looks through their phone at a Coke can, which, as I discussed in chapter one, was an augmented reality experience funded by Coke.

The next frontier of live sports may be immersive experiences without a headset or phone, like what's being done at Cosm. TMRW Sports, TGL Golf is another example where pro golfers compete in real tournaments using a combination of virtual and IRL (in real life) play. They tee off into a massive five-story screen the way you would at a golf simulator (but *way* larger) and then play on a green that exists in real space. All of this is set within an intimate arena that creates a completely new experience for fans. The green rotates and features nearly six hundred actuators embedded under the putting surface to change the way the green plays from hole to hole. As the athletes work their way through the course, the green rotates so fans can all get an equal view of the action without having to change their seats. It's a fascinating setup, with a format that allows for courses that could never exist in real life, like bespoke holes set in a giant canyon or floating on bodies of water.

For all the technology involved in delivering TGL, from the beginning, founder and CEO of TMRW Sports, Mike McCarley, has seen this as a media business. As Jon Kropp, TMRW Sports VP of digital media, put it, "Mike . . . is a marketer at heart. And he was constantly being nagged by how great a television sport golf is, how great a business professional golf is. And yet it's a great product despite so many inherent challenges . . . There's eighteen fields of play. The superstars are not often in the same frame on the television, right? You need to wait four days to get a result. And despite all those challenges, it was still a great fan product. And so . . . we get to start fresh and build the next generation media company [building on the success of traditional golf with new technology experiences]." Much like Cosm, TGL is about creating a new fan experience that is made for TV/digital media from the ground up. It starts with a physical structure that presents a traditional sport in an entirely new way, adding to the experience of the in-person fan as well.

Kropp highlights, "The arena is effectively broken into two halves . . . More like the design of a performing arts center than a traditional basketball or hockey arena, which is a full oval. At the open end of the horseshoe sits a screen that is sixty-four feet by fifty-three feet and what we like to call the world's largest golf simulator. The shots into the simulator start thirty-five yards back and the ball is tracked with . . . radar technology, which provides the inputs to that simulator. And then, similar to a golf simulator that you would see in an entertainment environment or at your home, the shot gets rendered via ball-tracking technology, but here's where it gets really interesting. The last sixty-five yards of our facility includes a physical green that we can manipulate. It rotates. We can change the undulation of it. So we can design different finishes for each hole. And the players then, when a ball lands within that footprint in the virtual world, the players then finish the hole in front of the crowd in the physical world. So we're going through the looking glass in two directions." The business is called TMRW Sports, not TMRW Golf, for a reason. More sports will follow.

Simulator Prequalification

For the last fourteen years, NASCAR has partnered with a company called iRacing to apply flight simulator technology to the racetrack. According to Tim Clark of NASCAR, "It is incredibly advanced software, real 3D telemetry scans of all the racetracks, so that you have essentially created as close to a life-life simulation of racing that you could possibly imagine . . . William Byron competed for a championship last year [he finished third in the standings in 2024] . . . Before he ever set foot in a race car, he was on iRacing. He tells the story of, after being so successful in iRacing, he convinced his parents to let him get in a race car. He basically couldn't go up the hill because he didn't understand the fundamentals of how to work the clutch. And then once he got going, he finished second in the race, just based on skills that he had refined on iRacing."

What makes NASCAR's approach cutting edge is not only the technology but also the way that they apply simulators as a path to qualify drivers. I predict that, as technology continues to evolve, more sports will create virtual experiences that overlap with live ones like we are seeing with TGL. Virtual technologies can allow people anywhere in the world to experience sports in new ways, and I'm interested to see how this area of sports technology evolves.

Optical Tracking Technologies

I recently asked Chris Benyarko of the NBA about which near-future technology he is most excited about. He said, "Technology around optical tracking and what that provides. I think that's one of the technologies that doesn't get much attention but has potential to have a lot of impact across our space. Optical tracking is vital to advancements in refereeing and officiating and getting calls right and getting them faster. So that improves overall game flow. Then also optical tracking is the foundational technology that allows us to do mixed and shared reality experiences. So being able to recreate game flow and experiences and put that into different worlds . . . I think optical tracking is a big piece that's going to help unlock that. I like to say it helps even on the side of efficiency. It's just impossible to put as many cameras as you would want across an entire arena. So, you need to think about other technologies that allow you to create a mesh or an overall view . . . If you force me to choose one [technology that will change sports in the next five years], I'll say optical tracking."

Optical tracking is advanced technology that uses a combination of computer vision algorithms and high-speed cameras to capture real-time data on athlete mechanics, projectile (i.e., ball) trajectories, and other match/race elements that would be impossible to capture and analyze without this technology.

To show what's possible, let's say I invent a product called MessiCam. If someone is a dedicated fan of football player Lionel Messi, they can buy a subscription to the MLS MessiCam and be able to view Messi wherever he runs on an MLS pitch, even if the primary broadcast coverage focuses on something else. The fan not only gets to zero in on their favorite player, but, when combined with historical data on things like *distance run* or *time on pitch*, fans and betting companies can begin to predict how he may perform for the rest of the match. As a note, every piece of the technology that would make this product possible is already here. The holdup exists mainly in what data should be public versus for internal use only and the way that public data could impact player value, predict injuries, etc.

ARTIFICIAL INTELLIGENCE AND GENAI

As of the time of this writing, nearly every conversation I have about the future of technology centers on one topic: generative AI (GenAI). It's worthwhile to make a distinction between AI in general, which comprises a large number of technologies, most of which use machine learning, and GenAI in specific. GenAI produces text, images, code, video, and additional outputs from prompts at scale. A few examples are ChatGPT from OpenAI (also called a large language model [LLM]), Google Gemini, Stable Diffusion, and Microsoft Copilot, but there are many others.

AI systems have been around in sports for years now. Some technologies add tags automatically, create basic analytics, and track player performance. WSC Sports and others have used AI to automate the clipping of highlights and turn longer content into additional short media assets. Marketers have used AI to generate personas and identify opportunities to create additional revenue from engaged fans. Very early GenAI generated basic articles from sports statistics and scoring. Advancements in GenAI since late 2024 have dramatically changed the game.

I am old enough to have been around for Web 1.0 in the mid-nineties, as the world introduced a paradigm that had not previously existed with the consumer internet. That experience informs what I expect to happen with AI and GenAI now. The sports industry and the world are currently just beginning to contextualize what the technology can do for business, just like in the early internet. But how tools and agents evolve remains in question.

The easy applications of GenAI are already clear: AI can generate images, text, code, and simple short videos. It can not only pull highlights from games but also create insights and analysis that would take a person many hours to create. It can take previously tedious workflows requiring lots of manual labor and streamline and automate them. It can even produce an AI agent that speaks to fans in ways that are difficult to distinguish from an actual human, replacing the need for human call centers. But the hard part for executives is to grasp the deeper applications of this technology. How can we contextualize how we should apply AI to enhance the *business* of sports? How can we leverage the technology most strategically?

AN EXPERT ON AI IN SPORTS

To help inform my discussion on AI and GenAI, I also talked with Shripal Shah, former chief strategy officer of the Washington

Commanders and author of *The Art of Victory: AI and the New Frontier of Global Sports* and *Leveling Up With AI: A Strategic Guide to AI in Sports Marketing*. We're fortunate that Shripal is now Next League's chief digital officer and is helping our clients imagine how sports organizations leverage these new technologies to acquire new fans and drive revenue. He's one of the leading experts on AI in the sports industry, and I wanted to hear what he had to say on how traditional and generative AI will both impact our field.

According to Shah, "Five years ago, when AI was in its infancy in sports, it was really focused on basic analytics, tracking player performance, early machine learning models for, say, injury prevention. Identifying engaged or unengaged season ticket customers. The industry was trying to explore AI potential, but it was more of a 'nice to have' than a strategic tool. I think where we are now, AI is becoming more integral to sports operations. When you think about how it's being used to personalize the fan experience, drive real-time analytics, and even predictive modeling . . . IBM Watson and the USTA US Open and Amazon AWS are powering the next-gen stats in the NFL."

Shah believes the adoption of AI will take two tracks that happen simultaneously. First, there will be the seamless changes. More and more applications will come in with built-in AI that makes the user more productive, creative, and able to do more, faster. That productivity boost will accelerate work across the field and decrease costs, without requiring much thought. For example, a ticket seller on SeatGeek now has the ability to "turn on" AI dynamic pricing to make more money on the secondary market without additional effort. Shah thinks there will be thousands of similar applications in the future.

Big Impacts in Marketing

Traditional, nongenerative AI has made substantial impacts on the retail and marketing arenas already, according to Shah: "It used to take someone two weeks to code an email blast . . . Now with the evolution of just the basic marketing software or SaaS tools out there, almost all organizations are finding that the timeline's gone from two weeks to as little as potentially two days or less. And they're doing it with less people . . . All the retailers are reducing their head counts, yet they're still getting more productivity. And it's because AI has really driven that."

That leap forward in productivity is already coming to sports marketing. Shah says, "I just read about NASCAR having built a similar marketing tech stack where they created a CDP on Snowflake and . . . created a layer where they now have over a thousand personas that they can use for personalized marketing . . . In the NBA, the Sacramento Kings were one of the first teams to really embrace the Salesforce marketing cloud in 2019 . . . They saw a 25 percent year-over-year increase in season ticket sales, because Salesforce was one of the original innovators in bringing traditional AI into their marketing cloud. So people who were just using the Salesforce marketing tools by default were getting benefits of AI features that the other marketing tools at the time just didn't have."

Generative AI tools in SaaS platforms already look poised to increase conversions on marketing emails for sports teams, according to Shah, by as much as an additional 7 percent.

In addition to the seamless changes, Shah thinks there will be AI applications for sports properties that require thought. Does the property want to automate a particular task or problem solution? What are the potential risks, and is the property willing to take them? The need for thought is a key part of how GenAI adoption will be different than mobile or social media adoption in years past. With social media, sports properties had to go all in, retraining as needed. With AI, the property may want to pick and choose, ensuring that the technology serves their goals, their risk tolerance, and who they are as an organization.

Katee LaPoff, OVG's CTO, agrees with Shah's assessment from the technical perspective of someone who's been in the industry for decades: "I tell people all the time, and this is an old Katee adage, all automation is doing all the hard work of thinking, planning, and programming upfront. If you don't have a good business process, if you don't have good data, if you don't have a good understanding of requirements and outcomes, all automation does is make you do stupid things faster. And I think AI can be the same thing. If you allow a machine to program itself with bad information, bad business processes, lack of requirements, and no controls, you'll get what you put into it, which is nothing good." She argues that thinking AI applications through is critical. "Now conversely, I think AI has an enormous amount of potential [if used with care in the right way]," LaPoff said, and I agree. Just as many software technologies require detailed thinking for effective automation, so do the more powerful applications of AI. In no way does the need for rigor undermine the power of the technology—if anything, it underscores it.

CONTENT CREATION

The most obvious application of GenAI for the sports industry is content creation. Rather than simply clipping highlights or creating additional shortform media from existing content, AI can now create new content from scratch. While many others point to open questions about the quality of the output, the ability to generate large quantities of content quickly cannot be understated as a value to sports organizations now, and the quality of the output will increase significantly over time.

Shah says, "ESPN had their ESPN Edge Innovation Conference and they were talking about using generative AI to create videos for many of the articles [that didn't have them] . . . to drive more engagement to their media channels. The idea of using AI to create original content [in the sports industry] is something that we're just starting . . . that's going to drive some new interesting areas for fans, but it'll also drive probably areas of concern or adjustments . . . If a major media entity is going to use AI to create original content, that's going to open the door for hits and misses. And I think that's going to then test the fandom's patience as they get used to this. This is really no different than broadcast bringing in social media." The potential for improvement is incredible, but new content creation should be approached cautiously.

Consider: Where does the fan demand for content outpace your team's ability to provide it? What parts of that content could be most easily done with AI? Here, as always, begin with small-scale experiments and pay attention to fan feedback as you go.

CODE GENERATION

GenAI technologies like Microsoft Copilot offer the ability for skilled software engineers to streamline the code creation process by automating rote work and suggesting potential code solutions in line. As I mentioned early in the book, the inaccuracy problem means that AI-generated code can at times be less accurate, with more errors than human-generated code, so quality-control practices become particularly important. That being said, GenAI creates significant time savings for software engineers, which leads to productivity increases, cost and timeline decreases, or both. The advancements in code written by AI mean that the quality of that code will shortly surpass the quality of code written by humans. It's one of many areas where machines should just perform better than humans.

If you code a significant amount of software in house, do not overlook the productivity gains and cross-language assistance that a tool like Copilot can offer. Most teams will see notable gains within a few months. In fact, the data says that your engineers are already using these tools whether you know it or not.

INFORMATION RETRIEVAL

Large sports organizations have massive amounts of business information, video footage, interviews, and statistics, among other sources of archived information. To locate the right media assets is difficult; up until now it has required extensive internal knowledge or specialty database query languages. No longer, with AI.

The NFL and Amazon recently partnered to use GenAI on just this kind of problem within the NFL. According to a recent article, they have developed an automated assistant "that facilitates access to business intelligence and production knowledge using natural language prompts," and created a system "for easy retrieval of insights and video footage [stored] in the Next Gen Stats dataset . . . Both will be used to help employees produce more and better content across its properties . . . Production assistants will be spared countless hours of manual tasks, such as watching video to tag plays, 'freeing up that human time to spend it back on the most valuable activities.'" *

* Lemire, Joe. 2024. "NFL, Amazon Web Services Extend and Expand Partnership and introduce generative AI for collaborative projects." *Sports Business Journal*, September 10, 2024. https://www.sportsbusinessjournal.com/Articles/2024/09/10/nfl-aws-extension.

Does your organization have enough internal content to make a specialized retrieval assistant worthwhile?

HOW LEADERS USE AI

Here are four sports technology leaders on how their organizations are using GenAI right now. Notice how many possibilities there are beyond retrieval, content, and code.

> **Chris Marinak, chief operations and strategy officer for MLB:** "Sports organizations are relatively small businesses, you know, compared to a bank or a major tech company. We just don't have the same level of resourcing, people, and investment. And so those are the areas where I think the GenAI piece can add a lot of value, whether it's improving the way that we reach fans with content, images, video. We've used software engineering tools to help us become more efficient at writing software code, and helping us speed time to market and create features more quickly. That's been a great use case for us . . . We've [also] been looking at things like translation. We're a global sport. Primarily obviously based in the United States and Canada, English speaking, but a ton of Spanish-speaking influence in baseball and even a lot of Japanese, Korean, other languages . . . Those are the kind of things that I think are showing real promise. I think they're still at the experimentation phase. And I think it's a little unclear how you use them, how often, and how high of a bar you need in terms of quality."

Shripal Shah, chief digital officer at Next League: "People are starting to test the use of AI to predict crowd noises and spikes to adjust advertisements . . . when there's a louder stadium reaction, right in the broadcast . . . That's the type of AI use that might be seamless or silent to the average fan, but it's going to be done so that Coca-Cola or Pepsi, if their advertisement may show up when the stadium is louder because they want to be associated with that fan moment. So when all the highlights and the social media and everything else goes, the logo and the advertisement in the background is associated with that predictive moment . . . Things like that I think are going to start coming really quick."

Perkins Miller, CEO of PlayOn Sports: "Yes, so we use AI both on sort of two fronts in the business. One is on product development and technical work. [And the other is just general productivity enhancement.] . . . There's some that are integrated directly into tool sets you would use, like a Copilot, for example, that allows a developer to sort of test code, load code, build code . . . People in HR, they need a quick jumpstart on writing a job description. Job description is done in three minutes as opposed to three hours. Someone who is working on video is looking for ways to think about graphics development . . . accelerated by 70 percent . . . We [also] do game guides today. We're going to be able to build things tomorrow that I think really help people play the game more easily, find what to watch more easily. That sort of stuff is going to make a real difference."

Jeff Price, CEO of the Heisman Trophy Trust: "The way we think about AI, certainly in the coaching space, is that it's going to enhance what the coaches are able to do, but the personal and human connection is going to be critical. The best coaches are going to have AI and technology helping them create better experiences. But the human relationship and the interaction between a coach and a player is really what we're focused on and how do we use that to help that relationship to grow . . . to make it a better consumer experience, better business opportunity for our coaches, their facilities, their employers."

As Price describes in the last quote above, the best uses of GenAI complement the human element rather than replace it. Tim Clark of NASCAR puts it this way: "[I think] the thing that [has been] pervasive in the conversations we've had internally is that we're not looking at AI or similar technology as a way to replace human beings, right? It's more of a supplemental tool."

As you consider using GenAI in your organization in new ways, where can your organization use automation and AI to *add* to human processes? Where can it replace those processes, and what can those people be freed up to do instead?

TIMELINE OF ADOPTION

Shripal Shah says AI is going to transform the industry much faster than previous technological revolutions: "The timeline it took for social media from 2008, 2009, when Twitter started to turn. It was sort of this fringe thing to . . . commentary broadcast. That took almost ten years. I think the curve for AI might be a third of that." I agree, and if anything, I believe that Shah is underestimating the speed of adoption. The cost savings alone will drive sports organizations to invest heavily in this technology.

As Shah puts it, "The more teams start embracing AI, they're going to be able to do more. They're going to find . . . where things that might've taken three thousand hours are now taking less than a hundred. So when you think about the cost savings, that's what's going to really lead to the unlock. It may not be AI itself that does it. But if AI can reduce something that takes three thousand hours to a hundred hours . . . that's when the magic's going to happen."

AI can be a driver of immense efficiency gains, to the point that it seems well worth its risks and limitations.

RISKS AND LIMITATIONS OF CURRENT AI

Here is some perspective on the biggest limitations and risks of mainstream GenAI models, as currently described by technology leaders and AI experts.

- **Automation risk.** As Katee LaPoff pointed out, all automation requires careful thought to prevent it from simply making "you do stupid things faster." Take the time to ensure machines reason from good information, take strategically useful steps toward your goals, and have controls on their use.
- **Software sprawl.** Unless carefully planned from the beginning and continuously reigned in during builds,

the humans in charge of software create a tendency for that software to sprawl. New licenses are added but not tracked. Feature after feature can get added without planning, and the sum of the parts doesn't add up to as much as it should. Because GenAI accelerates code creation, it can also accelerate this tendency for organizations that are not careful to fight it.

- **The inaccuracy problem.** Based on their large datasets and sources, all traditional GenAI models available at the time of this writing generate some percentage of inaccurate results and will need to be corrected by "humans in the loop" before being shown to fans.
- **You may need to train your own model.** The value of the sports brand is so important that you cannot deliver inaccurate information, so building your own model may be necessary to control inaccuracy issues at the source. If a proprietary model is solely trained on licensed, cleaned, accurate sports data, the inaccuracy goes down dramatically. The model is only as good as what you train it to do, and that reality carries with it costs.
- **Reproducing bias.** As Shah points out, all AI will reproduce whatever patterns and biases exist in the data sets it was trained on. He points to a study by UMass Amherst of historical sports broadcast commentary and how minority quarterbacks are described in terms that we would find offensive today. If an AI model is trained on sixty years of broadcast commentary, the output it produces may reflect bias in a way that causes issues.

The most important principle is that you only get out of a model what you put into it, both in terms of data set and prompting. The models will tend to reinforce and accelerate good decision-making but also do the same with poor decision-making, so care is needed in execution.

AI AS AN AGENT, AND THE FUTURE

As I said earlier, I believe we are still early in the adoption curve of AI in the sports industry. Our current level of AI and GenAI are "narrow," limited models. If someone asks a model a question, it will give a result, or an answer. The answer is often different from prompt to prompt, which makes the system different from traditional software, but it won't deviate from the original request. The latest AI models are being built now as agents, rather than tools, technology that can act independently to, say, make trip reservations or change calendar entries after a single prompt, rather than simply speeding up steps of human action. For technology to be able to act as an agent is a massive step forward, and one we don't yet understand the full implications of.

AI experts say that the models are likely to increase in intelligence dramatically in the next few years. This next step of artificial general intelligence (general AI) may be able to think logically and even philosophically, equaling or outstripping humans in most tasks. The systems may be able to understand differences between things that currently stump AI and reason about those things with a degree of agency and nuance. This higher level of AI could replace humans in complex jobs and would change every aspect of society.

The next step beyond general AI is superintelligence, where AI will think about things that we don't understand. If this type of AI evolves, it will have true agency, look at the conditions around it, and make decisions it will then carry out without human input. At that point, the Pandora's box is open, and we don't yet know what will come out. But while General AI seems likely to evolve, super-intelligence may or may not, and in any case, will have implications we can't yet plan for.

In 2025 a group of esteemed AI experts[*] penned a well-researched blog post outlining the way they believe things will unfold from mid-2025 through 2027.[*] Basically, this post is a scenario that represents their best guess about what that might look like. It starts this way: "We predict that the impact of superhuman AI over the next decade will be enormous, exceeding that of the Industrial Revolution."

They go on to describe the way AI will evolve, including the version of agent (described as Agent-1) that by early 2026 ". . . knows more facts than any human, knows practically every programming language, and can solve well-specified coding problems extremely quickly. On the other hand, Agent-1 is bad at even simple long-horizon tasks, like beating video games it hasn't played before. Still, the common workday is eight hours, and a day's work can usually be separated into smaller chunks; you could think of Agent-1 as a scatterbrained employee who thrives under careful management. Savvy people find ways to automate routine parts of their jobs." The entire post is worth reading, it's eye opening (and more than a little frightening).

---

* https://ai-2027.com/

THE FUTURE

Technology is a train that is not going to stop. If you ignore the train, it will leave you behind. If you choose the right train, monitor its direction, and stay along for the ride, you can harness its momentum and progress for your own ends.

No one knows the future, but everyone knows that change is coming. The manner of that change may disrupt the way that you make money today. We saw this with live venue events drying up overnight in the pandemic, a massive disruption to the sports industry where, for many large leagues, 40 percent of the revenue comes from ticket sales. Postpandemic, people are coming back to sports venues. They are enjoying many experiences that were developed because of the pandemic, which have accelerated our ability to get people into venues and keep them safe. The world will continue to change. Some change will be technology reacting to the ways humans behave, and some will drive the way humans behave.

Kodak was the biggest company in the world when it came to film, but the advent of digital photography left them behind. The tragedy wasn't inevitable. According to some reports, they had developed the first self-contained digital camera, but they refused to undercut their physical film business. BlackBerry had the same response to the release of the first iPhone. They decided to double down on what made them different and unique, and that was the wrong choice.

Pay attention and be willing to adjust to the changes as they happen. Monitor new technologies, experiment, and invest.

THE FUTURE: ACTION LIST

Apply the lessons of this chapter by considering the following actions:

- **Review your strategic work** from the first five chapters. How does your north star and identity as an organization guide how you should approach newer technologies?
- **Consider new technologies.** Spend some time thinking through the new technologies presented in this chapter as well as any you have read about. Which, if any, should you test in your organization?
- **Train for AI use** within your organization, and **develop policies for use.** What are use cases that can help move your business forward? Can you use it in content, code, or retrieval? Are there other possibilities? Are there internal rules that should govern use to limit risk and liability?

CONCLUSION

Success or failure in sports technology is rarely about the choice of the technology itself.

Of course, it *is* possible to choose technologies that will not accomplish your goals. A Phillips-head screwdriver will never be a hammer, no matter how fervently you swing it. Identifying the appropriate technologies for the need will matter, especially as the technology landscape continues to evolve over time. If the technology delivers what is needed for the required business outcome, and the commercial terms make it viable, you will usually be faced with a set of reasonable options. These foundational decisions aside, what is far more important is the strategic thinking. How will the technology be deployed and maintained in practice, and over time?

In my opinion, a sports executive's role isn't to live on the cutting edge of technology, but rather to continuously improve strategy to achieve the organization's goals and decide how or if that strategy should change year to year. Then, the executive should obtain good counsel (experts in technology), either within or outside of the organization, to help inform specific technology research and execution as needed. Let them advise you on the details and focus your efforts on the strategic direction and choices to get there.

Innovation has value in and of itself but should at least have the possibility of translating into business value. But being first is less necessary than not being last. Moving in the right direction is more critical than doing what is trendy if what is trendy isn't right for your strategic outcomes.

Technology is becoming mission critical to every aspect of a sports organization. It is increasingly accelerating progress against all our goals, year over year. Sports organizations have always wanted to sell more tickets, for example, and AI-driven technologies are making that goal dramatically faster and easier to obtain. But without clear thinking, we only accomplish the wrong things faster. We waste more effort. We repeat ineffective actions over and over with automation. So, in a time of ever-increasing, ever-more-powerful technology and artificial intelligence, it's never been more important to think carefully and strategically.

Don't drop the ball at the two-yard line. Hire or engage competent people to advise, research, and implement and help you choose your technology carefully and strategically, in keeping with your goals. If you choose to look for additional help externally, choose someone without a dog in the fight, who knows the sports industry and who is not looking to sell you any specific product.

The Competencies Model I have outlined here works, no matter how you select and deploy technology. When executed effectively, the right ***counsel*** supporting strategic decision-making and proper ***choices*** aligned with your business goals, a transparent and accountable ***governance*** framework for technology leadership, and the empowerment of talent to consistently ***execute*** through repeatable processes will steer your organization toward success. Define your goals, develop your strategy, make good choices, and execute well.

I would be negligent at this point not to mention that Next League fits that criteria. We think first about strategy and business outcomes and only second about technology tools. We work for you, and we're committed to your success, not selling technology. Perhaps most importantly for the sports industry, we have fine-tuned the process of implementation over years to land on time and on budget. We understand (and deliver) the uncompromising timelines of the sports industry because we work for no one else.

While almost 90 percent of sports organizations pursue some form of digital transformation, fewer than 30 percent achieve meaningful ROI on these efforts. With advanced analytics and AI-driven personalization, your organization can deliver measurable revenue growth, deeper fan relationships, and results up to three times faster than traditional approaches.

By starting with a competencies model like the one I've outlined here, you can make intelligent technology *real*.

The train is leaving the station; will you be on it?

#KNOWWHATISNEXT

ACKNOWLEDGMENTS

My wife, Jeanine, is my best friend and the most caring and loyal person I have ever met. She's an amazing mother to our three great kids, and any success I've had is directly connected to our partnership. When my mom suddenly passed seven months after we were married, and the responsibility of caring for my disabled sister, Anne, suddenly passed to two newlyweds, not a word was spoken about what needed to be done. Not a word. Jeanine immediately facilitated how we would ensure that Anne would have a place in our new home, no matter where that might be. Over twenty-five years later, we still care for Anne. Thank you for sharing your life and being the purpose of mine.

To my kids, Reece, Hudson, and Tess, I could not be prouder of who you are. I'm excited for the journey that lies ahead of you. Thanks for inspiring me.

To Chris Marino, the man of limitless energy and enthusiasm, best friend, and brother-in-law, thank you for family and friendship.

To Andrew Siegel, your counsel and friendship mean more to me than you know.

To Pete Aquilone, who is no longer with us, your kindness changed my life. Thank you.

To Doug Perlman, thanks for answering my call that afternoon when you were at the barbershop. My life would have been different without that call and your friendship. I still enjoy our long talks. It's been quite a ride.

To the OMNIGON and Next League team members, you are the smartest and best team in the business of sports technology. You all made me better every day and are my extended family. Thank you for your conviction and talent.

To Krishnan Ramachandran, you are a true professional, and I'm lucky to call you a friend.

To Becki Civello and Joanna Solowey, you are my friends and the best at what you do. Thank you for filling my gaps.

To Igor Ulis, Mike Grushin, and Bora Nikolic, the smartest and most talented people I have ever met or worked with, thank you for your friendship and years of fighting and winning. I've learned a tremendous amount from all of you and look forward to what is next.

To the literally hundreds of other staff and business relationships, including those who contributed their thoughts to this book, including Tim Clark, John Martin, Brian Herbst, Katee LaPoff, Mollie Marcoux Samaan, Liz Moore, Mike McCarley, Jon Kropp, Kara Baker, Adam Freifeld, Jon Podany, Amanda Weiner, Dave Giancola, Sarah Hirshland, Katie Bynum Aznavorian, Rob Simmelkjaer,

Chris Benyarko, Chris Marinak, Devin Poolman, Shripal Shah, Joe Leccese, Brad Ruskin, Rob Freeman, Corey Leff, Dan Mannix, Jeff Price, Nicole Jeter West, Clark Pierce, Ryan Kuttler, Scott Gutterman, Luis Goicouria, Paul Johnson, Amy Scheer, Jayne Bussman-Wise, Marc Jenkins, Perkins Miller, Pete Vlastelica, Matteo Perale, Alessandro Albanese, and many, many others—thank you all.

There are many, many others who deserve thanks. Please know that I appreciate it and hope I can continue to show that I deserved it.

To Abe Madkour and the entire *Sports Business Journal* team and Amplify Publishing including Naren Aryal, Myles Schrag, and, *especially*, Alex Hughes Capell, thanks for your support in bringing this all to life.